Tobias-Georg Schmidt

***

Founding Limited Companies in Germany

Perspectives and Risks

www.salzwasserverlag.de

Schmidt, Tobias-Georg

Founding Limited Companies (Ltds) in Germany

Perspectives and Risks

1. Auflage 2007

ISBN-13: 978-3-937686-67-7

Nachdruck, auch auszugsweise, nur mit schriftlicher Genehmigung des Verlags

© CT Salzwasser-Verlag GmbH & Co. KG, Bremen/Hamburg, 2006 (www.salzwasserverlag.de)

Druck und Herstellung: Hohnholt Reprografischer Betrieb GmbH, Bremen (www.hohnholt.com)

Dieser Titel unterliegt dem Gesetz zur Regelung der Preisbindung von Verlagserzeugnissen (BGBl. I Nr. 63 vom 5. September 2002)

Die Deutsche Bibliothek verzeichnet diesen Titel in der Deutschen Nationalbibliografie. Bibliografische Daten sind unter http://dnb.ddb.de verfügbar.

Table of Contents

Table of Contens	I
Table of Figures	III
Index of Abbreviations	IV
Table of Annexes	VI
Explanations on Vocabulary Issues	VII
1. Introduction	1
2. History of Companies in Britain	3
3. Overview of English Types of Companies	6
4. Developments in EU Legislature	10
4.1. Background	10
4.1.1 Freedom of Establishment	10
4.1.2 Real Seat Theory	10
4.1.3 Incorporation Theory	11
4.2 Daily Mail	12
4.3 Centros	13
4.4 Überseering	14
4.5 Inspire Art	15
4.6 Intermediate Results	17
5. Establishment of a Limited	19
5.1 The Required Persons	19
5.2 The Process of Establishment	19
5.3 Management Bodies of the Limited	21
5.3.1 The Director or the Board of the Directors, respectively	21
5.3.2 The General Meeting	23
5.3.3 Company Secretary	24
5.4 Registered Office	25
5.5 Regulations on Capital	25
5.5.1 Raising the Limited`s Capital	25

5.5.2 Maintenance of the Limited's Capital	27
5.5.2.1 Capital Reduction	27
5.5.2.2 Repurchase of Own Shares	28
5.5.2.3 Distributions to Shareholders	28
5.5.2.4 Governmental Supervision	28
5.6 Liability of Shareholders and Managing Directors	29
5.7 Transfer of Shares	30
5.8 Accounting, Audit and Disclosure in England	31
5.8.1 Accounting	31
5.8.2 Audit	32
5.8.3 Regulations on Disclosure	33
5.9 Taxation and Insolvency in England	35
5.9.1 Taxation in England	35
5.9.2 Insolvency in England	36
6. The German Branch Office as the Company's Administrative Seat	38
6.1 The German Branch Office	38
6.2 Registration of the Branch Office	40
6.3 Permanent Representative	43
6.4 Liability in the Branch Office	44
6.4.1 "Kapitalerhaltungshaftung"	45
6.4.2 "Existenzvernichtungshaftung"	46
6.4.3 "Insolvenzantragspflicht" and "Insolvenzverschleppungshaftung"	47
6.5 "Mitbestimmung"	48
6.6 Transfer of Shares in the Branch Office	49
6.7 Accounting, Audit and Disclosure in the Branch Office	50
6.8 Taxation of the Branch Office in Germany	51
6.8.1 Taxation on the Limited's Level	51
6.8.2 Taxation on the Shareholder's Level	52
6.8.2.1 The Limited's Distribution of Profits to Shareholders	52
6.8.2.2 Sale of Shares in the Limited	53
6.9 Insolvency of the Branch Office in Germany	53
7. Perspectives and Risks of Establishing a Limited in Germany	57

7.1 Advantages of the Limited Compared to the GmbH	57
7.2 Disadvantages and Risks of the Limited Compared to the GmbH	59
7.2.1 Current Costs	59
7.2.2 Legal Uncertainty	61
7.2.3 Creditworthiness	62
7.2.4 The German Register of Companies	63
7.2.5 Acceptancy	65
7.3 Chances and Perspectives of the Limited	66
8. Conclusion	68
Annex 1	IX
Annex 2	X
Bibliography	XI

Table of Figures

Fig. 1: Overview of English Company Types	6
Fig. 2: Flexibility of Capital Raising	26

Index of Abbreviations

AGM = Annual General Meeting
AO = Abgabenordnung (≈ Fiscal Code)
Art. = article
BB = Betriebs Berater
BGB = Bürgerliches Gesetzbuch (≈ German civil code)
BGBl = Bundesgesetzblatt (≈ Federal Law Gazette)
BGH = Bundesgerichtshof (≈ Federal Court of Justice)
BStBl = Bundessteuerblatt (≈ Federal Tax Gazette)
BV = Besloten Vennootschap met beperkte aansprakelijkheid (equivalent to a Limited Company in the Netherlands)
CA = Companies Act
CLR = Company Law Review
DB = Der Betrieb
DKK = Danish Krona
DStR = Deutsche Steuerrichtlinien
DTA = Double Taxation Agreement
EC = European Community
ECJ = European Court of Justice
ECJ = European Court of Justice
EEA = European Economic Area
EGBGB = Einführungsgesetz zum Bürgerlichen Gesetzbuch (≈ Introductory law to the German Civil Code)
EGM = extraordinary general meeting
EGV = Europäischer Gemeinschaftsvertrag (Treaty of the European Union)
EStG = Einkommenssteuergesetz (Income Tax Act)
et seq. = and the following
EU = European Union
EuInsVO = Europäische Insolvenzverordnung (European Council Regulation on Insolvency Proceedings)
EWGV = Vertrag zur Gründung der Europäischen Wirtschaftsgemeinschaft (Treaty of the European Economic Community)
Fn = Footnote
FRG = Federal Republic of Germany
GAAP = generally accepted accounting principles
GB = Great Britain
GBP = British Pound
GewStG = Gewerbesteuergesetz (≈ local Business Tax Act)
GmbH = Gesellschaft mit beschränkter Haftung
GmbHG = GmbH-Gesetz (German Limited Liability Company Law)
GmbHR = GmbH-Rundschau
HGB = Handelsgesetzbuch (German Commercial Code)
HRV = Handelsregisterverordnung (≈ order on the setup and management of the register of companies)
INF = Informationen über Steuern und Wirtschaft
InsO = Insolvenzordnung (Insolvency Code)
KG = Kommanditgesellschaft
KStG = Körperschaftssteuergesetz (Corporation Tax Law)
LTD / Ltd. = Private Company Limited by Shares

MDR = Monatsschrift für Deutsches Recht
MindestKapG = Mindestkapitalgesetz (≈ Minimun Capital Law)
NJW = Neue Juristische Wochenschrift
p = page
p. et seq. = page and following
pp. = pages
PLC = Public Company Limited by Shares
RdW = Recht der Wirtschaft
RIW = Recht der Internationalen Wirtschaft
Sec. = section
Sent. = Sentence
SolZG = Solidaritätszuschlagsgesetz (≈ solidarity surcharge law)
Subsec. = Subsection
UStG = Umsatzsteuergesetz (≈ Value Added Tax Act)
VAT = Value Added Tax
w/o = without
WFBV = Wet op de formeel buitenlandse vennootschappen
WM = Wertpapier - Mitteilungen
WStH = Wirtschafts- und Steuerhefte
ZGR = Zeitschrift für Gesellschaftsrecht

Table of Annexes

Annex 1   Form 10 – First Directors and Secretary and Intended
           Situation of Registered Office   IX

Annex 2   Form 12 – Declaration on Application for Registration   X

Explanations on Vocabulary Issues

In English company law, there are two general types of companies: partnerships and companies.

Actually, there are several meanings of the term 'company': the first one, generally speaking denotes the entire spectrum of associations that may be set up to do business. Thus, this comes closest to the German "Gesellschaft".

The second 'company' is most like the "Kapitalgesellschaft". Its definition is narrower and therefore more clear. This points to those types of companies in English company law in which liability is limited to the investment made by the shareholder. In fact this is the main distinction of partnerships. Such businesses are called 'limited liability companies' in British English. The Companies Act 1985 regards the public limited company and the private limited company as two different variants, which have the same basic legal structure, as well as the same statutory requirements. There are just a few differences, the most prominent being the circle of shareholders. While this circle is restricted in the private company, this is not the case in the public company.

The German business forms of "GmbH" and "AG" are two distinctive legal forms in German company law. However, in their function and economic importance, the "GmbH" is practically the equivalent of the private company, while the "Aktiengesellschaft" (AG) is very similar to the public company (Güthoff 1993, 4).

In order to avoid misunderstandings in connection to the technical terms of this paper, I will briefly discuss a few key terms:

Company – in the broader sense [≈ Gesellschaft]

joint-stock company – historic, British English term for companies in which shareholders could invest, but did not yet have limited liability

Limited liability company – British English term for stock companies with limited liability [≈ Kapitalgesellschaft]

Public company, PLC – public limited company [≈ AG]; "AG" is used when the German "Aktiengesellschaft" is discussed

Limited, Ltd., LTD – private company limited by shares or private limited company, [≈ GmbH]; "GmbH" is used when the German "Gesellschaft mit beschränkter Haftung" is discussed

Several German technical terms have no English equivalent, mainly because these matters are not common in English law. The terms are explained in the text. The German term will then be used in the text to avoid inexact or misleading translations. The following terms provided as translations are merely constructs that, in my opinion, are pretty close to the overall meaning of the German term:

Existenzvernichtungshaftung ≈ liability in case of destruction of existence
Insolvenzantragspflicht ≈ duty to file for insolvency
Insolvenzverschleppungshaftung ≈ liability due to obstruction of insolvency
Kapitalerhaltungshaftung ≈ capital conservation liability
Mitbestimmung ≈ workers' co-determination
Eigenkapitalersatzregeln ≈ concept of equitable subordination
kapitalersetzende Gesellschafterdarlehen ≈ shareholder loans that replace equity capital
Kapitalersatzrecht ≈ law on equitable subordination

1. Introduction

In a globalized Europe in which everything is merging together, especially the economies, and keeping pace with the rapid development of the Internet, one can ill afford not to take a look at the Limited company.

The English Limited seems to be an alternative to the German GmbH. In the course of groundbreaking decisions, made by the European Court of Justice, a new legal platform for economic activity is made available in Germany. So far, it seems to be an attractive one.

The fast and uncomplicated establishment of the company, as well as the rather liberal rules of capitalization, are typically perceived as advantages of the Limited compared to the German GmbH.

However, the limited – being a foreign type of company – is, first of all, an alien element in the German legal system (Just 2005, Preface).

There are many questions to be answered and there is, additionally, a certain amount of legal uncertainty to be reasoned with concerning the decision of whether or not to choose the limited over the German GmbH.

Also, the peculiarities, perspectives and risks of the limited are widely unknown to the general public.

The purpose of my work is to provide an analysis of how an English private company limited by shares based in Germany may offer an alternative to German forms of business organization for entrepreneurs. The perspectives and risks that come hand in hand with such an establishment will also be interpreted.

To begin with, I will shortly explain the history of British companies.

This is then followed, firstly, by an overview of the types of companies in England, and, secondly, the two types of businesses known to British company law in which liability may be limited to the paid-in company assets. A discussion of the new rulings of the European Court of Justice (ECJ), followed by the topics of freedom of establishment, incorporation theory and real seat theory are also presented. The next chapter explicitly examines establishment and management of the limited according to English company law. In general, a branch office of the foreign company is established to engage in business in Germany. This process, as well as the taxation and the applicability of German law on this branch office are discussed in the following section. The subsequent chapter focuses on the perspectives and risks, as well as the advantages and disadvantages of a limited operating in Germany, before a final conclusion is drawn.

2. History of Companies in Britain

The earliest 'companies' in British history were the medieval guilds and the livery companies of London. Essentially, they were trade associations that regulated the relevant issues in their respective professions, e.g. the wages of apprentices or quality standards for their products and merchandise.

Later on, the ages of Mercantilism and trade imperialism saw the emergence of the modern company's precursors, at a time when risky but promising ventures needed extensive funding. It was, for instance, the search for a north-east passage to Asia that prompted the foundation of the first major English joint-stock trading company. This was the Muscovy (or Russia) Company, which was given a monopoly on the Russian trade (www.encyclopedia.com (a)). In 1568, the first inland joint-stock companies in England were founded. These were the Mines Royal and the Mineral and Battery (www.ex.ac.uk). As a financing model, the joint-stock company allowed companies to raise large amounts of capital and to lower the risk by spreading the capital over several ventures (http://en.wikipedia.org (a)).

Joint-Stock companies, as a type of business, flourished in Great Britain until the early 18th century when the country experienced a huge setback through the collapse of the South Sea Bubble. The South Sea Company set up a scheme to take over the country's national debt in exchange for its own stocks, expecting to make a considerable profit in the transaction. The government's approval resulted in a wave of speculation, and many dishonest, speculative ventures sprang up. When the bubble burst in 1720 thousands were ruined, among them members of the government (www.encyclopedia.com (b)). Consequently, Parliament passed the Bubble Act. It banned all joint-stock companies not authorized by royal charter, and prohibited the creation of any new joint-stock companies that did not have Parliament's expressive approval. The ban remained on the books for 105 years (http://en.wikipedia.org (b)).

As it was lifted in 1825, the concept of limited liability was introduced into legislation. However, this applied only to chartered companies.

The various types of modern companies in Britain today have their origins in the nineteenth century. William Gladstone is considered the true father of the modern company. As President of the Board of Trade, he introduced the Joint Stock Companies Act of 1844.

The acquisition of corporate personality was extremely difficult and expensive up to that time, since it could be achieved only by Royal Charter or under the provisions of a special Act of Parliament. The Joint Stock Companies Act now provided for the giving of corporate identity (incorporation) by registration.

The Act also clearly distinguished between companies and partnerships. However, it did not yet include the limitation of liability (www.hmrc.gov.uk (a)).

This was introduced by the Limited Liability Act of 1855, which allowed companies to limit the liability of their individual investors to the value of their shares. Beforehand, they stood to lose all their wealth in case the company was driven out of business. The curtailing of risk that was made possible by the act is evidently the basis for the increased investment in trade and industry in the second half of the 19th century (www.bbc.co.uk).

The full implications of the legislation on limited liability were recognised as late as 1897, in the decision of the House of Lords in Salomon v Salomon & Co Ltd. As a result of the Companies Act, 'One-man' companies became common for the first time, although the public regarded the founders of such companies to be hiding behind the façade of corporate identity, especially in the case of failure. The House of Lords reversed former decisions by the Court of first instance and the Court of Appeal stated that the business was the business of the company, and not of Salomon. This implied a clear legal distinction of the company and its subscribers. In other words, the company is not the agent of its members (www.hmrc.gov.uk (b)).

In 1862, the 'modern' company law was codified in the Companies Act of 1862, which is the forerunner of today's Companies Act. It consolidated the important developments in legislation at that time (www.hmrc.gov.uk (c)).

Partnerships, besides joint-stock companies, constitute the second main group of company types. The Partnership Act of 1890 laid a cornerstone, providing the basis for the liability of the general partner, much like in German law. In 1907, the Limited Partnership Act followed, defining the rights and obligations of the limited partner (Scamell 1962, 799).

In 1908, the Companies Acts from 1862 to 1908 were consolidated and in 1929, a new Companies Act then consolidated the amendments of the 1908 legislation. Further amendments, but also new provisions were passed in 1948 and in 1967. In the 1970s and 1980s many reformations in company law were made in order to compete with the requirements of the European Community legislation (www.hmrc.gov.uk (d)).

Today, the applicable company law is the Companies Act 1985 and the updating legislation contained in the Companies Act 1989 (www.companieshouse.gov.uk (a)). In 2000, the Limited Liability Partnership Act introduced a further company type. The next chapter will provide an overview of the various forms.

3. Overview of English Types of Companies

There are a number of types of companies in English company law, such as, for example the partnership, the private limited company, the public limited company, the European Economic Interest Grouping, and the European public limited company, as well as companies by law or by concession to the crown (Just 2005, 2). The English company law divides its types of companies into sole proprietorships (single or sole Trader), partnerships, companies and special forms of organisation for certain lines of business (Güthoff 1993, 1 et seq.). The following figure offers an overview of English company types.

Fig.1: Overview of English Company Types

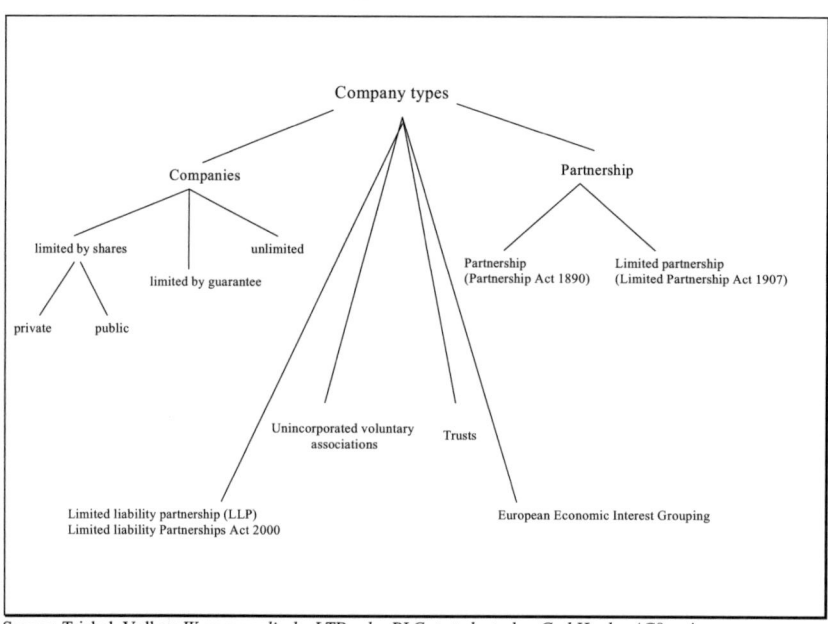

Source: Triebel, Volker: *Warum englische LTD oder PLC statt deutscher GmbH oder AG?*, p.4

Partnerships and companies will now be the focus of attention.

There are two types of partnerships in English law, namely the general partnership and the limited partnership, which differ in the liability of their respective entrepreneurs. In the general partnership every partner is personally and unlimitedly liable. In the limited partnership on the contrary, the liability of one or more partner(s) - but not all - is restricted to the amount they have invested at the time of its establishment (Güthoff 1993, 1 et seq.).

The general partnership is an association of at least two persons that have the intention to realise profits through engaging in business activities. It is often compared to the German "Offene Handelsgesellschaft", but is, in fact, not equal to it, since an engagement in business is not an explicit requirement of the general partnership (Güthoff 1993, 1 et seq.).

Due to the existence of general partners and limited partners, the limited partnership is, instead, regarded as equal to the German "Kommanditgesellschaft" (Güthoff 1993, 1 et seq.).

The limited partnerships in England have very little significance, for, in contrast to Germany, the legal requirements for the establishment of a limited liability company are relatively minimal. Therefore, even the smallest companies prefer limited liability companies as a type of business (Güthoff 1993, 1 et seq.).

The limited partnership is most often taken into account when individual partners merely want to invest their capital without having to assume the full liability for debts and liabilities of the company (Güthoff 1993, 52).

Among the types of companies known to British company law there are two types in which the liability can be restricted to the paid-in company assets (Dierksmeier 1997, 83). They are called "Private Company Limited by Shares" and "Public Company Limited by Shares". There are also "unlimited companies", in which a partner's liability is *not* limited and thus includes his private fortune.

The following abbreviations have gained acceptance in referring to the types of companies in which liability may be limited to paid-in business assets:

Legally correct designation	Common abbreviations
Private Company Limited by Shares	LTD, Limited, Limited Company
Public Company Limited Company	PLC

The company capital is divided into shares in both company types. Therefore, they are both corporations.

The distinction lies in their respective shareholder circles, usually understood because of the labels "private" and "public". The Private Limited Company has a restricted circle of shareholders, whereas the shares of the Public Limited Company are free to be distributed to a broader public.

The British company law is regulated in the "Companies Act". It applies to the LTD and the PLC. Special laws on forms of business organizations, such as the German "GmbH-Gesetz" [German Limited Liability Company Law] or the "Aktiengesetz" [German Stock Companies Act] are unknown. If one uses the shareholder number as a comparison criterion, the British and German companies may be characterized as follows:

Shareholder number	British form of business organisation	German form of business organisation
Restricted	LTD	GmbH
unlimited	PLC	AG

Essentially, the British PLC corresponds to a German "Aktiengesellschaft". In economic terms, it is the most important company type in Great Britain (Güthoff 1993, 52). Public companies are obliged to fix a minimum share capital of £50,000. A quarter of its par value with premium is also supposed to be paid in immediately. However, working with this type of company outside of Great Britain makes sense only in individual terms. The implementation of the British LTD, on the other hand, closes a gap that has been left open in German company law. It offers a complete limitation of liability even to small businesses and entrepreneurs. A private Company is not subject to the regulations of the minimum share capital. Yet, it is illegal to sell its shares or debentures to the public. The company's capital is provided privately, same as it is in a German GmbH (Triebel, Hodgson, Kellenter 1995, 216). A conversion of a private company into a public company, or vice versa, is possible at all times in Great Britain. As it is not mandatory to posses a minimum share capital and the legal requirements concerning its establishment are rather small, the LTD represents the prevalent type of company in Great Britain (Güthoff 1993, 52).

The Companies Act 1985 [1] has introduced the type of limitation of liability as an additional distinctive feature. Liability is, first of all, either limited by shares (as mentioned above) or, secondly, through a sum of guarantee.

In the case of a possible termination, the partners of a „Company Limited by Guarantee" are only partly liable for the company's debts. The amount is fixed in the Memorandum of Association[2]. „Companies Limited by Guarantee" are especially useful for activities in which profit-making is not directly intended, e.g. in non-profit organisations. (Just 2005, 3).

---

[1] Registration is the most common form in order to set up a company in England. This can take place either on the basis of European regulations, or based upon national laws with different governmental authorities. The most important law is the 1985 Companies Act. Other laws are the Building Societies Act 1986, the Charities Act 1993, the Friendly Societies Act 1992, the Industrial and Provident Societies Act 1965, the Limited Liability Partnerships Act 2000, and the Open-Ended Investment Companies Regulations 1996.

[2] The Memorandum, being the most important document in the foundation of a company, has to include, besides the name and the seat of the firm, the limitation of liability and the amount and partitioning of the nominal share capital, as well as a declaration as to the purpose of the company.

4. Developments in EU Legislature

4.1. Background

4.1.1 Freedom of Establishment

Articles 43 to 48 of the EC – Treaty regulate the freedom of establishment throughout the European Union. Freedom of establishment allows legal entities or companies to establish in a Member State of the EU, as long as a stable and permanent integration into the economy of the said state can be ensured. A legal entity is subject to this law if it has been established under the national law of a Member State, *and* if its head office is also situated in a Member State (http://de.wikipedia.org).

Hence, companies are allowed to carry out key economic activities in other Member States of the European Union.

Due to the considerable differences between the national company laws of different Member States concerning the provision and conservation of capital, the establishment, organisation and control of companies as well as the internal and external liability of the shareholders and the managing directors, and additionally the protective rules for creditors, investors and the market, one cannot speak of a common European company law (Horn 2004, 893). Through respective jurisdictions, the single EU member states have developed their own theories for the interpretation of the European Community Law. Especially those national company law arrangements, that are consistent with the Community Law have resulted in contradictory opinions, that currently are being discussed as real seat theory and incorporation theory.

4.1.2 Real Seat Theory

In Germany, the Articles of Association of a foreign company, which define its internal and external relations, were derived from the company law of the Member State in which the administrative seat (or real seat) of the company was located (Korts 2004, 26).

This approach was known under the term real seat theory and was applied by German jurisdiction until well into 2002. Companies that had been established under foreign law, but had their actual administrative seat in Germany, would not be registered and were thus not acknowledged as a legal entity in Germany. Besides Germany, France, Belgium, Luxembourg, Portugal and Greece also applied the real seat theory (Korts 2004, 27). The focus of the real seat theory lies in protective interests (Bayer 2003, 2358).

4.1.3 Incorporation Theory

The matter is somewhat different with the incorporation theory. The choice of which company law is to be applied is left up to the founders. This is possible by the nomination of a formal company domicile. The applicable law then depends on the location stated in the Articles of Association, or the location of registration (Vogel 2005, 212).

The headquarter's location (real seat) is irrelevant in this context, meaning that it does not have to be the same location as the formal company domicile.

Nevertheless, certain connections to the law of the (host) state are being integrated, through which the state is granted minimum control, much like in the real seat theory. In Great Britain, for example, all companies are subject to rigid control rights in order to ensure the protection of creditors (Korts 2004, 27).

The incorporation theory has the advantage of a clear legal position and thus leads to stability and unlimited legal acknowledgement of the established company in all legal systems that follow this theory (Bayer 2003, 2358).

Advocates of the incorporation theory are Great Britain, Denmark, the Netherlands, Switzerland and Spain (Korts 2004, 27).

The European Court of Justice has reached several ground-breaking decisions concerning the incompatible views of the application of the common law. These decisions are further examined in detail.

4.2. Daily Mail

The "Daily Mail" act, called for by the ECJ on September 27, 1988 (ECJ 9.27.1988 – Case 81/87), tread the case of the Investment company "Daily Mail and General Trust PLC", which had been established under English law, and – out of tax-related reasons – moved its formal seat to the Netherlands, while the actual administrative office and the statutory seat remained in Great Britain (Bayer 2003, 2359).
The investment company attempted to avoid the taxation of undisclosed reserves, which, according to British law, would have occurred in the subsequent selling of considerable parts of its assets, supposed to yield substantial capital gains (Bayer 2003, 2359). The English treasury denied the company the permission to relocate. This was later acknowledged by the ECJ.
This confirmed the opinion of the German jurisdiction that proclaimed that the real seat theory was to be applied with companies that had been established in other EU Member States as well (Bayer 2003, 2360).
Literally, the ECJ stated:

[...] unlike natural persons, companies are creatures of the law and, in the present state of Community law, creatures of national law. They exist only by virtue of the varying national legislation which determines their incorporation and functioning. (ECJ, 9.27.1988 – Case 81/87)

"Articles 52 and 58 of the Treaty [now Arts. 43, 48 EC], properly construed, confer no right on a company incorporated under the legislation of a Member State and having its registered office there to transfer its central management and control to another Member State." (ECJ, 9.27.1988 – Case 81/87)

"Daily Mail" was a case of relocation from one state which applied the incorporation theory (Great Britain) to another state (the Netherlands). This meant that the question of consistency of the real seat theory with the Common European Law was not even at issue. This fact had been noticed in Germany, but was not considered to be of much importance (Bayer 2003, 2360).

4.3 Centros

As a result of the outcome of the March 9th, 1999 "Centros" case (ECJ, 3.9.1999 – Case C- 212/97), the ECJ considered the registration denial of an English company's branch office in Denmark to be an unjustified restriction of the freedom of establishment as provided by the Community Law (Korts 2004, 28).

As a matter of reference, it is the following that led to this decision: A Danish couple established and registered a private limited company in Great Britain, naming it "Centros Ltd.". However, the company's subscribed capital of £100 was not paid in, as the English law does not require this (Korts 2004, 28).

The plan was to not get involved in any business in Great Britain, but rather to do business exclusively in Denmark (Bayer 2003, 2360). By establishing a Limited in Great Britain, the Danish company law would be avoided, since it required a minimum share capital of DKK 200,000 when founding a company with limited liability (Korts 2004, 28).

However, the Danish authorities were "not amused" and denied registration of the business as a branch office, claiming that it was, in fact, not a branch, but a main office. Therefore, the business had to meet the requirements of the Danish company law and, in particular, those concerning the minimum share capital (Bayer 2003, 2360).

According to the freedom of establishment, Articles 43 and 48 of the EC - Treaty, the ECJ then forbade the Danish authorities the denial of registration (Vogel 2005, 212).

According to the ECJ, the freedom of establishment was restricted because a company that has supposedly transferred to another Member State would then become subject to the state's company law, which was unknown and perhaps even stricter. The Company would, consequently, have to be newly established following the regulations of the host Member State.

Through this ruling, the freedom of establishment was expanded. From this time onward, it also included dummy foreign companies (Horn 2004, 895). Furthermore, it stated that the assessment of possible abuse has to be carried out with loyalty to the Common law, rather than to the respective national law.

The ECJ also took a stand as to how far restrictions of the freedom of establishment are justifiable. The following four cumulative requirements were, however, not fulfilled in this particular case. The requirements are as follows: measures "are to be applied in a non-discriminating manner, […] be justified by mandatory reasons of public interest, [...and] be suitable for reaching the pursued aim. [...Furthermore,] they should not exceed what is necessary in reaching this aim" (Probst, Kleinert 2003, 1268). This "four-criteria-test" has gained recognition under the name of "Gebhardt-Formula".

By virtue of the "Centros-ruling", the ECJ has withdrawn the basis for the real seat theory that had been applied in German jurisdiction, even if only for cases of a company transfer *to* a country, and not for cases of transfers *from* a country (Vogel 2005, 212).

4.4 Überseering

With the "Überseering"– decision of November 5th, 2002 (ECJ, 11.5.2002 – Case C-208/00), the ECJ granted full legal capacities and suability after home law to a Dutch company whose main administrative office was located in Germany (Triebel, von Hase 2003, 2409).

The said case concerned a company that was registered in the Netherlands as "Besloten Vennootschap" (BV) (Überseering B.V.), which carried out business from Düsseldorf. When the company raised claims of guarantee against a building contractor, it was told that it did not have legal capacity or suability. The courts' rationale was that the company's substantial seat was in Germany and thus it was subject to German company law. However, it had failed to meet the applicable German regulations of establishment and, therefore, did not exist in legal terms (Vogel 2005, 212). Restrictions of transfers away *from* a country did not play a role in this decision, since the Netherlands do not recognize such restrictions. The only restrictions that were examined by the ECJ were transfer restrictions *to* a country. The decision, then, was that it is a violation of the freedom of establishment, as guaranteed by articles 43 and 48 of the EC - Treaty, for another Member State to not acknowledge the legal capacity and suability of a company it is entitled to by law of establishment (Triebel, von Hase 2003, 2409).

The ECJ's decision made it clear that all legal systems of the European Union are fundamentally respectable and of equal value (Korts 2004, 35).

The ECJ made up for the delimitation to "Daily Mail". The explanations in "Daily Mail" concerning possible restrictions to transfers *from* a country were delimitated from restrictions to transfers *to* a country (Bayer 2003, 2361).

4.5 Inspire Art

A further step that opened the way for freedom of establishment in Europe was undertaken by the ECJ's ruling in the case „Inspire Art" of September 30th, 2003 (ECJ, 9.30.2003 – Case C-167/01).
Following the verdicts in the "Centros" and "Überseering" cases, the ECJ ruled in favour of companies' freedom of establishment for the third time in five years. As a result, the ECJ allowed for unrestricted competition between the different types of companies in Europe Wachter 2004, 89 (a)). Therefore, every European company is free to do business in its state of domicile, and that unaltered, according to the law of its State of establishment, which is based upon the freedom of establishment provided by the Treaty. This also accounts for any case in which there may be stricter requirements to capital resource in the State of domicile than in the State of establishment (Riedemann 2004, 345).

The "Inspire Art" case is about a limited established in Great Britain that sold art pieces and supplies. A few days after incorporation, it took up business in the Netherlands - the same place as the sole director's domicile, who registered the firm's branch office with the Amsterdam Chamber of Commerce (Kersting, Schindler 2003, 621). However, the branch office was registered without the rider that it was formally a foreign company. This rider would have been necessary, according to the "Wet op de formeel buitenlandse vennootschappen" (WFBV, Law about formally foreign companys and dummy foreign companies, respectively) as of December 17th, 1997 (Staatsblad 1997 Nr. 697).
In spite of repeated requests by the Chamber of Commerce, the company failed to register this adjunct. Thus, the ECJ had to decide whether the Dutch law on dummy foreign companies was compatible with the European freedom of establishment.
Though the Netherlands was fundamentally clinging to the incorporation theory, they enacted the WFBV in order to avoid the passing-by of mandatory regulations of the

Dutch company law by the establishment of foreign companies (Wachter 2004, 89 (a)).

Accordingly, all foreign companies are deemed dummy foreign companies if they run their entire, or biggest part of, the business in the Netherlands, without being in possession of any substantial connections to the State that they were established in (Wachter 2004, 89 (a)).

According to law, registration should depend on the following criteria:

1. Registration as a "formally foreign company",
2. Mention of the date of the first registration and information on the sole shareholder in the register,
3. The characteristic of being a formally foreign company is to be mentioned on all documents,
4. The subscribed capital has to be at least the same amount as the minimum capital that is mandatory for Dutch limited companies, which is €18,000, and
5. Personal liability of the managing director for the debt of the company as soon as the company does not dispose of the required capital either at the time of establishment or at a later date (Maul, Schmidt 2003, 2297).

Finally, the ECJ ruled that it was irrelevant to the application of the freedom of establishment *why* someone would found a company in another Member State, or *where* it conducts its business (Korts 2004, 40).

Moreover, the required additional registration and the adjunct on the business letters and documents of the company were more than what was necessary (Wachter 2004, 90 (a)).

Additionally, the regulations of the WFBV are an impediment to the freedom of establishment, since they result in the imperative application of Dutch company law, concerning the minimum capital and liability of the managing directors, to foreign companies, such as Inspire Art Ltd (Korts 2004, 40).

Justifications for the limitations of the freedom of establishment were not recognized by the ECJ, as national law may impose limitations only in the following cases:

1. For the protection of creditors,
2. for the integrity of commerce,
3. in the prevention of an abuse of the freedom of establishment,
4. in the fight of fraud,
5. for the effectiveness of tax controls,
6. in the protection of public law and order (Wachter 2004, 90 (a)).

4.6 Intermediate Results

Correctly already since the Überseering ruling, but at the latest since Inspire Art, the ECJ has refused each and every limitation of possibilities to move into a country for companies that have been established inside the EU. Therefore, the real seat theory has become obsolete, while the ECJ took a fundamental stand in favour of the incorporation theory in the cases of company transfers *to* other Member States (Bayer 2003, 2363).

In this context, Probst und Kleinert advocate protective mechanisms which EU-lawmakers should implement for all states, in order to prevent abuse, passing-by and dummy firms (Probst, Kleinert 2003, 1268).

The previous German custom of considering foreign companies as "offene Handelsgesellschaften", or "Gesellschaften bürgerlichen Rechts", respectively, has become obsolete due to the ECJ's decision. Foreign limited liability companies are to be acknowledged as such in Germany (Just 2005, 5).

However, the influence of the law of incorporation can only be considered from the scope of the EC - Treaty and the EEA - Agreement. Meanwhile, in relation to third-party states, the common law tie of the actual administrative seat of the company remains as long as there are no intergovernmental treaties to the contrary (von Bernstorff 2004, 500).

It must be mentioned that the ECJ, because of its ruling in the case "de Lasteyrie du Saillant" of March 11th, 2004 (ECJ, 3.11.2004 – Case C-9/02), also considers restrictions of transfers *from* a State to be inadmissible, at least if connected to a change of residence.

In determining admissibility tests of transfer restrictions *from* a country, the same criteria are used as those that were authorized by the ECJ in the test for justifications of restrictions of transfers *to* a country. Tax-related, or other restrictions of transfers *from* a country, are therefore admissible only in very few circumstances (Probst, Kleinert 2004, 2425).

5. Establishment of a Limited

The establishment of a Limited can occur in two distinct ways: by establishing a new company or through the acquisition of a shelf company.

The latter option is preferred if a certain company is to be acquired as fast as possible. Many providers of services for Limiteds offer shelf companies or assume the establishment (Just 2005, 7). This is the usual procedure for German founders. Some of these offers include the provision of a secretary (cp. item 5.3.3) and a registered office (cp. item 5.4).

5.1 The Required Persons

When establishing a new limited in Great Britain the following persons are needed:

- One shareholder,
- one director, and
- one company secretary.

Since the shareholder may additionally hold the post of director or secretary, the establishment of a limited requires at least two persons. Usually, only the positions of shareholder and director may be held by one and the same person. If secretarial services are externally bought, a „Single Member Company" is possible (www.companieshouse.gov.uk, (b)).

5.2 The Process of Establishment

Four documents must be submitted to the responsible register, namely the Companies House in Cardiff:

- Memorandum of association,
- Articles of association,
- Form 10 – First directors and secretary and intended situation of registered office (cp. annex 1), and

- Form 12 - Declaration on application for registration (Just 2005, 7). (cp. annex 2).

Together, the "Memorandum of Association" and the "Articles of Association" constitute the articles of incorporation.
Under the Companies Act 1985, the two documents have to comply with the forms specified by the Secretary of State (Ebert, Levedag 2003, 1337).
The "Memorandum of Association" covers the company's external relations to third parties. It defines legal minimum standards, amongst them, the following:

- Name and seat of the company, along with the adjunct "Limited",
- the company's object,
- type of liability of the shareholders,
- division of the share capital into shares and nominal value, and
- count of shares acquired by each founder (Vogel 2005, 213).

The "Articles of Association" constitute the second part of the articles of incorporation. According to these articles, the internal relations of the company and its shareholders and management may be regulated on a voluntary basis (Vogel 2005, 213).
If the articles are not submitted to the register, the regulations, which are stated in the annex to the Companies Act 1985 as Table A, automatically replace them as the articles of the company (Werner 2005, 288). Table A models articles for public or private companies limited by shares (Ebert, Levedag 2003, 1337).
The articles cover everything from the rights of the directors to the constitution and authority of the board of directors and the procedure of general meetings, to the rights and prohibitions of voting (Güthoff 1993, 20).
"Form 10 – First directors and secretary and intended situation of registered office" (cp. annex 1) represents a standardized form containing information to be submitted to the register: name and address of the company, of its directors and secretary with their names, dates of birth, addresses, nationalities and professions (Just 2005, 8).
"Form 12 – Declaration on application for registration" (cp. annex 2) requires a statutory declaration stating that the company is to be established under the

regulations of the Companies Act 1985 and that legal regulations have been met (Just 2005, 8).

According to the Declaration of Compliance, either a solicitor, director or company secretary must state that all legal requirements concerning registration have been met (Werner 2005, 289).

The registrar of the Companies House then makes sure that the company's name – which must end in "Ltd." or "Limited" to denote the legal form – is already in use by another company or not. It must also be confirmed that the company's statutory object does not violate any laws.

If both prerequisites are met, the firm is enlisted in the index of firms and is assigned a registration number. The Memorandum of Association is then issued (Ebert, Levedag 2003, 1338).

It usually takes three days to set up a limited. However, paying an extra charge allows for an establishment within 24 hours (Bauhoff 2004, 827).

Additionally, a company's name may easily and quickly be changed.

5.3 Management Bodies of the Limited

5.3.1 The Director or the Board of Directors, respectively

The English limited as a legal entity requires representative bodies that act on behalf of the company in legal relations. The directors, who make the decisions in business affairs and conclude contracts for the company, assume this function.

The Companies Act 1985 obliges every Limited to nominate at least one director (Section 282 CA 1985). The Articles of Association specimen even calls for at least two directors (Table A, article 64). If Table A has been adopted at the time of establishment, but only one director is nominated, an amendment of the statutes is imperative (Just 2005, 29).

The Articles of Association regularly oblige the director to simultaneously hold a share of the business.

Normally, the directors of a Limited hold at least the majority, if not all of the shares of the company. In many cases, the articles either appoint the directors for life, or for at least a three-year period. There is no limitation of age (Güthoff 1993, 46).

In principle, the directors are entitled only to a joint management and representation. However, if the articles provide for it, the "board of directors" may present single directors with certain authorities (Triebel, Hodgson, Kellenter 1995, 268).

The distinction between executive and non-executive directors among board members is an English peculiarity. Contrary to German law, which allows for no combined administration and control authority, both functions are united in the English board. The non-executive directors' task is to guarantee the company's interests. However, non-executive directors are frequently found in public companies (Just 2005, 30).

The (executive) director's obligations to the company include:

- Fiduciary duties: loyalty towards the company, acting "in good faith for the best interests of the company",
- disclosure of one's own interest in a contract or in holding a share of the company,
- obligation to act in due care when acting in the company's interest, and
- timely notification in case of insolvency (Maul, Schmidt 2003, 2298).

Furthermore, the director is also responsible to the Companies House for the orderly and punctual submission of the following documents to the English register:

- Accounts,
- tax return,
- annual return, and
- annual balance sheet (Go Ahead Limited, 15).

A director might as well be forbidden per verdict to further function as managing director. Reasons leading to such a disqualification are:

- Abuse of company fortune,
- disregard of company interests resulting in damage to creditors,
- repeated violations of statutory public disclosure regulations,
- fraudulous actions connected to an insolvency, and

- criminal offences (Maul, Schmidt 2003, 2299).

Minors, foreigners and legal entities may occupy the position of a director (Heinz 2004, 15).

5.3.2 The General Meeting

The most important body of an English limited is the general meeting, which is composed of the individual shareholders, and holds the company's entire power of decision. It is comparable to the general meeting of a German GmbH, which also represents the supreme body of the company (Dierksmeier 1997, 40).

The director, or the board of directors, respectively, may convene a general meeting at any time and for any purpose. In this meeting, every shareholder, even the director, or the directors respectively, are allowed to participate and to exercise their right to speak. However, the directors are allowed to vote only if they are shareholders at the same time (Just 2005, 20).

The annual general meeting allows shareholders to question the directors on matters of business development and to discuss the annual financial statement (Just 2005, 20).

According to Table A, the general meeting also allows for the determination of the dividend and the election of directors and auditors. Agenda items, such as the re-election or voting out of directors, the payment of a dividend, the explanation of the balance sheet and the discussion of company strategies, are passed by a simple majority.

All English companies are required to hold at least one annual general meeting (AGM). However, according to sec. 366 A CA 1985 a private company is not obligated to hold such a meeting (Güthoff 1993, 46), as this represents an unnecessary formality, since shareholders and directors are oftentimes a single person in private companies.

Besides the annual general meetings, extraordinary general meetings (EGM) may also be held. EGM is the term for every other general meeting, which is usually convened by a director. In certain rare cases a shareholder can also convene them (Just 2005, 21). In an EGM, the necessary shareholder's decisions are carried through. Among other things, this includes decisions on increase of capital, decisions on amendments or changes to the Articles of Association or the company's name (Goldstein, Wulferding 2004, 43).

5.3.3 Company Secretary

Every company is obliged to nominate a secretary, who is not required to possess special professional qualification (Güthoff 1993, 63).

The secretary ensures the compliance of the business' formalities and checks up on the correspondence with the register. A secretary's main responsibilities are administrative. If the tasks he has to fulfil demand it, he is also authorized to represent the company. The secretary's duties are monitored by a managing director or, in the case of a sole managing director, by an external third party (Sec. 283 CA 1985) (Werner 2005, 288).

The secretary has to implement the management's instructions. He, or she, is further responsible for the preparation of agendas and the maintenance of all meeting records, both extraordinary and general meetings (Just 2005, 44).

The secretary must keep track of management decisions and refer back to them on a regular basis.

Additionally, the secretary has to keep the following statutory books up to date:

- Register of members,
- directors and secretaries register,
- directors' interest (List of shares and loans of the managing directors with the company),
- register of charges, and
- register of minutes (protocol of managing directors' decisions) (Goldstein, Wulferding 2004, 49).

Much like the post of director, the post of secretary may be held by a foreigner or a legal entity (Heinz 2004, 16).

Smaller companies tend to consider the legal requirement of nominating a secretary a burden, rather than a facilitation.

Therefore, the Company Law Review[3] suggested to eliminate this requirement. It also suggested that, although the tasks should be considered an obligation, it should not be imperative that they be performed by an appointed secretary (Just 2005, 45).

5.4 Registered Office

In establishing a limited an address must be nominated as the "registered office" in order to enable the post office to deliver important documents and possible legal actions (Maul, Schmidt 2003, 2298).

At this address, the entrepreneur additionally has to keep ready certain documents for inspection by anyone and at any time during business hours. These documents include those that have been submitted to the Companies House, as well as a register containing all directors, shareholders and all further (required) information. The address is required to be in England. A company carrying out most of its business in Germany is, nevertheless, required to maintain this office, even if it is merely a post box. Maintaining the registered office results in current costs, as does the forwarding of mail to Germany, which also incurs risks of delay and loss (Happ, Holler 2004, 735).

As previously mentioned in item 5, many service providers take over the mandatory storage and forwarding of mail.

The registered office must be included on every invoice and business paper; the German branch office may be mentioned additionally (Go Ahead Limited, 15).

5.5 Regulations on Capital

5.5.1 Raising the Limited's Capital

This subsection begins with a graphic that shows the flexibility of raising the limited's capital.

---

[3] The *Company Law Review* was brought into being with the aim of rendering the English company law more competitive and fit for the 21st century by creating a simpler, cheaper and up-to-date framework for economic activity. Among its contents is a deregulation for small and medium-sized firms, which regularly choose the *private company limited by shares* as their form of business organization.

Fig.2: Flexibility of Capital - Raising

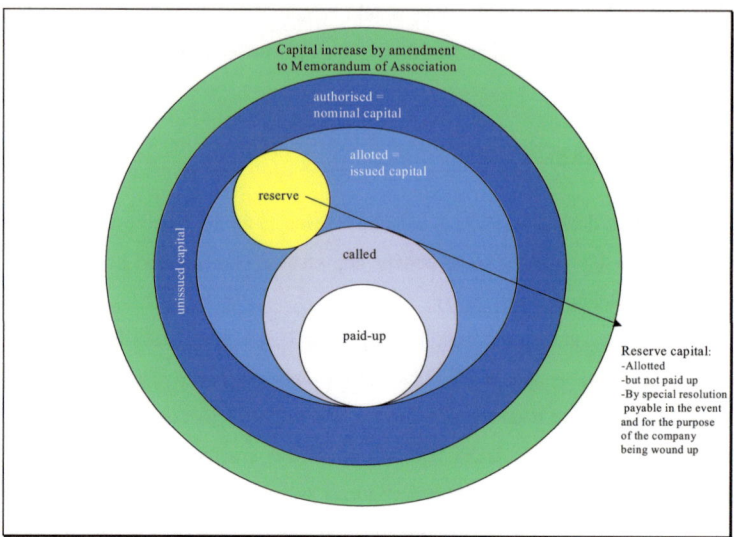

Source: Triebel, Volker: *Warum englische LTD oder PLC statt deutscher GmbH oder AG?*, p.10

One of the reasons most frequently mentioned for choosing a limited is the extremely flexible regulations concerning the raising of capital. According to the English Companies Act 1985, one may to establish a limited without a minimum share capital, but the limited would then be subject to severe public-law rules of surveillance and disclosure (Ebert, Levedag 2003, 1343). In theory, a limited may be equipped with a subscribed capital of £1. Practically however, a subscribed capital of at least £100 is paid in to one of the company's accounts (Bauhoff 2004, 826). The "nominal capital" mentioned in the memorandum cannot be compared to the subscribed capital of a German GmbH, but rather to the authorized capital of a German "Aktiengesellschaft" (Schumann 2004, 743). It merely represents a forecasted figure with the total amount of shares the company is allowed to issue (Triebel, Hodgson, Kellenter 1995, 235). The portion of the capital that has, in fact, been issued and is therefore very similar to the subscribed capital of a German GmbH, is described as the "issued capital" (Schumann 2004, 743). The issued capital denotes the sum of the shareholders' deposit liabilities and thus represents the company's liability coverage (Triebel, Hodgson, Kellenter 1995, 238). Shareholders are liable up to the nominal value of their subscribed shares (Triebel, Hodgson, Kellenter 1995, 238). If the nominal capital amounts to £100, but only two shares of

£1 each have been issued, the shareholder incurs a loss of only £2. The gap between the nominal capital and the subscribed capital is the so-called unissued capital (Just 2005, 46), while the capital that is actually paid in is called the paid-up capital. The eventual difference between the paid-up capital and the subscribed capital is described as unpaid or uncalled capital, respectively (Just 2005, 46). All in all, the term "uncalled" refers to the call of the company that is put down in the Articles of Association on a regular basis (Just 2005, 46). A shareholder can produce any capital-forming benefit as a deposit (Schumann 2004, 743). According to Sec.99, 106 CA 1985 the subscribed capital may be provided in cash or kind at the establishment. Sec.98 CA 1985 also allows for services to be considered as a type of cash deposit. The deposits are to be announced to the Companies House's registrator. However, a check of value is not conducted (Kallmeyer 2004, 637), unless the value seems illusory (Triebel, Hodgson, Kellenter 1995, 238). Deposits may be legally challenged only in the case of law abuse. Thus, there is no comprehensive value control with the English limited as there is with the German law on GmbHs. The assessment is instead left to the shareholders themselves (Just 2005, 46).

5.5.2 Maintenance of the Limited's Capital

The maintenance of capital is given greater consideration by British legislature than the raising of the capital. Maintenance of capital is also not handled as liberally as it is done in Germany.

The English law assigns the following regulations that govern the maintenance of capital:

1. Capital reduction,
2. repurchase of own shares,
3. distribution of dividends to shareholders, and
4. Governmental supervision (Schumann 2004, 744).

5.5.2.1 Capital Reduction

If an English limited possesses a share capital, then a confirmation by a court is required for reducing this share capital, according to Sec. 135 CA 1985. In the court's decision the creditor's interests are also covered, according to Sec. 136, 137 CA 1985. Under certain circumstances, creditors may successfully object to a reduction of capital (Schumann 2004, 744).

5.5.2.2 Repurchase of Own Shares

Principally speaking, a repurchase of one's own shares is inadmissible, according to Sec. 143 (1) CA 1985.

Exceptions are classified in Sec. 159, 162 (1) CA 1985. A repurchase of one's own shares therefore depends on whether the purchase is being financed using distributable profits or whether it is sustained using revenue that has been realized through the issuing of new shares (Schumann 2004, 744).

Another possibility is the assurance of the limited's managing directors that the company will still be able to meet their liabilities after the repurchase. This is generally described as "payment out of capital" (Schumann 2004, 744).

5.5.2.3 Distributions to Shareholders

According to Sec. 263 (1) CA 1985 only distributable profits may be paid to shareholders.

Furthermore, these profits may be used for distribution only after clearing them with loss carryovers (Kallmeyer 2004, 637). The distributable surplus is, according to Sec. 263 (3) CA 1985, the difference between the realized profits and losses.

This fact is particularly noteworthy for its long tradition in Great Britain.

Ever since 1882 (Flitcroft's Case), payments to shareholders may only be paid out using realized profits, since the subscribed capital is not to be undermined by repayment of deposits to the members.

5.5.2.4 Governmental Supervision

The limited is required to disclose the capitalization to the register on a yearly basis. Creditors to the company, as well as the British Ministry of Trade and Commerce, are entitled to request the legal liquidation of the company due to insufficient capital. In evidence of any unlawful or fraudulent business conduct should be found, government supervision might step in (Schumann 2004, 744).

5.6 Liability of Shareholders and Managing Directors

Presumably, one of the limited's most attractive characteristics is the fact that liability is restricted to the company's fortune. The shareholders' liability for debts and liabilities of the company is, more or less, ruled out. This limitation of liability has been a part of English law since the so-called Salomon – doctrine of 1897 (cp. item 2) (Heinz 2004, 18).

There have been a few exceptional cases, however, in which English law has provided for a lifting of the corporate veil (Vogel 2005, 214). The following groups of cases are especially important:

- *Agency:* a principal is liable for the legal transactions of his agent, who carries out those transactions in his own name and on his own account, but acts merely as a front man.
- *Fraud:* the company's existence in itself represents a bogus transaction, or the company has been established solely for law-abusing or fraudulent purposes (Ebert, Levedag 2003, 1340).

Since the shareholders' restriction of liability to the amount of their paid-in capital is rarely opened up, the focus of interest is shifted to the company's managing directors.

A director's personal liability may be the result of a violation of his loyalty and due care obligations, which have been mentioned in point 5.3.1. Besides this, liability exists due to the principles of *fraudulent trading* (Korts 2004, 45).

This term stands for a company's transactions that have been executed on fraudulent intentions. A director is, therefore, liable if there is an approaching insolvency and it can be proven that he intentionally acted contrary to the creditor's interests (Sec. 213 Insolvency Act 1986). However, it is rather rare and difficult to prove this (Maul, Schmidt 2003, 2299).

Furthermore, wrongful trading is also problematic (Sec. 214 Insolvency Act 1986). *Wrongful trading* is defined as negligent misconduct of the company, leading to the creditors' damage (Korts 2004, 45).

Accordingly, a director is to be held responsible after the opening of bankruptcy proceedings if he was, or should have been, aware of there being a sensible chance of avoiding the company's insolvency, and had, despite his knowledge, not undertaken every measure in order to minimize damage to the creditors (Maul, Schmidt 2003, 2299). With this, directors are obliged to monitor the company's financial situation throughout its entire existence. A managing director can avoid being held liable personally only if he convinces the court he had undertaken all steps to minimize the possible losses of the company's creditors (Schumann 2004, 747). A liability due to material underfunding, as may be found in Germany, is alien to an English understanding of law (Heinz 2004, 19).

5.7 Transfer of Shares

Shares in a private limited are freely transferable if the company's articles do not restrict transferability (Güthoff 1993, 46). A transfer of shares is accomplished by the shareholder selling his shares or handing them over to another person.
A private limited by shares is not allowed to sell shares publicly (Just 2005, 54).
Generally, shares are not transferred by a conveyance that is to be signed by both the transferor and the transferee, but on a stock transfer form, signed only by the transferor (Just 2005, 54). An authentication is not required. The company has to issue a new share certificate to the new shareholder on his name within a two month period and is also obliged to make a note of the new shareholder's name in the list of stockowners (Just 2005, 55). If the new shareholder is one of the directors at the same time, he is to notify the company of his acquisition of shares within five days. The alteration of the company's composition is to be reported to the registrar on the annual return (cp. item 5.8.3) (Just 2005, 55).
In the case of insolvency or a shareholder's death, the shares are passed on to a legal successor without further legal action (Just 2005, 55).
Since the transfer of shares is an internal process of the company and the real seat theory is generally acknowledged for all EU companies, it is indifferent whether or not the English limited's administrative seat is in Germany. In both cases, the transfer of shares is exclusively subject to English law (Heinz 2004, 25).

5.8 Accounting, Audit and Disclosure in England

5.8.1 Accounting

Regulations pertaining to the accounting of the English limited businesses include commercial bookkeeping and retention duties, as well as the obligation to prepare the annual accounts (Ebert, Levedag 2003, 1339).

The most important principle in balancing is the reproduction of a true and fair view of the affairs of the company at the end of each financial year (Just 2005, 61).

Aside from the question whether or not the administrative seat is to be found in England or Germany, the company is required to prepare annual accounts at the end of each financial year. The annual accounts contain a balance sheet, a profit and loss account with notes, a directors' report and the auditors' report (Just 2005, 61). The company is free to decide which one of two balance sheet formats (single-column or double-column echelons) it prefers. The company must also choose any of the four possible formats for the profit and loss account (Triebel, Hodgson, Kellenter 1995, 278).

Certain balance sheet items have to be separately explained in detail. This includes, among others, the list of market - and book values of fixed assets, as well as the total sum of income, pensions and compensations of all the directors (Triebel, Hodgson, Kellenter 1995, 280). As far as the profit and loss account is concerned, one has the option of choosing between the classification of expense by type and the classification of expense by function.

There are certain facilitations for small and medium-sized limiteds. In preparing the balance sheet, it is not an absolute requirement that all formalities are included. A simplified version of the annual accounts may also be submitted (Just 2005, 62).

In order to be regarded as a small or medium-sized limited company, two characteristics must to be met, according to law.

A company is considered a small limited company, if

- the annual turnover does not exceed £ 5,6m,
- the balance does not exceed £2,8m, and/ or
- the company does not have more than 50 employees (Just 2005, 63).

A company is considered to be a medium-sized company, if

- the annual turnover does not exceed £22,8m,
- the balance does not exceed £ 11,4m, and/ or
- the company does not have more than 250 employees (Just 2005, 63).

Threshold values have been raised accordingly, due to the Company Law Review's recommendation. So they have been valid since the end of January 2004.

In addition to the balance sheet the company's directors are obligated to present a business report to the general meeting. The purpose of this survey, which is comparable to the German status report, is to convey a summary of the economic situation during the specified financial year. Its contents are comprised of such: changes to fixed assets, the total amount and the breakdown of the turnover, shares held by directors and the number of employees, along with the total amount of their wages (Just 2005, 63).

5.8.2 Audit

In principle, every English company is obliged to have their books or annual accounts examined (Sec. 235 CA 1985), with the exception of inactive (or dormant) companies, as well as the relatively small ones. Since the end of March 2004, the threshold values for this category have been fixed as follows: an annual turnover of under £5,6m along with a balance of under £2,8m (Just 2005, 63).

If a company is subject to examination, the auditor is elected by the general meeting, in the case that the right has not previously been assigned to the directors. If no new auditor is chosen, last year's auditor is automatically reappointed (Just 2005, 63).

Only individuals and auditing companies that do not hold a post in, nor are employees of the company, may be nominated as auditors (Just 2005, 63). Someone who is not a partner or an employee of a director, secretary, or another employee, may also hold the post of auditor.

A additional prerequisite is the authorization of auditors by the "Secretary of State", which acknowledges auditors belonging to a professional association that is recognized in the United Kingdom. Foreign auditors that are appropriately qualified and provide evidence of sufficient knowledge and experience are acknowledged, as well (Triebel, Hodgson, Kellenter 1995, 281). The auditors' tasks include the supervision of the company's balance sheet, its profit and loss account and the director's business report. The auditors check whether or not these documents have been accurately prepared and if they convey an adequate reproduction of the situation of the given financial year. The auditors are then obligated to report their findings to the annual general meeting. This makes them responsible for the important function of supervising the directorate (Dierksmeier 1997, 43).

5.8.3 Regulations on Disclosure

The administration of a limited is complicated by the multitude of regulations on disclosure, which stipulate the deposit of documents and registration. The English legislator attempts to provide proper protection for investors and creditors through the strict requirements of disclosure, which allow for a more effective assessment of the company's creditworthiness. This enables them – if necessary - to call for more securities or to even refrain from the contract altogether. These requirements represent a balance of the rather liberal regulations on raising the capital.

In order to raise capital for a more extensive period of time, English companies rely on the public via the capital market, whereas in Germany, banks usually act as intermediaries between companies and investors (Triebel, Hodgson, Kellenter 1995, 276).

Within the ten months following the end of the financial year, the directors must submit all annual accounts, the business report and the auditors' report to the company register. There, everyone has the opportunity to inspect it (Güthoff 1993, 73).

A fine must be paid in the case that this obligation is violated and a civil law penalty for the company, the secretary or director may incur (Güthoff 1993, 73). The Companies House monitors compliance in reporting duties much more closely than the German register. In a final move, the Companies House may delete a company from the register because of a violation of reporting duties (Heinz 2004, 18).

Furthermore, the limited has to submit the annual return to the register on a yearly basis. This document must include the firm and address of the company, the name and address of every director and company secretary, current amounts of the nominal capital, subscribed capital, the paid-up and the receivable capital, current amounts of called-in deposits and issued debentures, as well as the registered charges of the company's assets (Just 2005, 64).

There is a host of further announcements that are tied to a time limit. Copies of certain resolutions must be submitted to the Companies House within 15 days. Any changes of the given information in the register concerning the directors or secretary, as for example a move or a change of profession, must be reported within 14 days. This time limit also applies to changes in the registered office's address. The allotment of new shares has to be reported within one month after any alterations (Heinz 2004, 18).

After having paid a small sum, the following critical documents of the company may be inspected at the registrar of the Companies House:

- Memorandum,
- Articles of Association,
- a directory of the subscribed shares,
- agreements on allotments in exchange for non-cash benefits and special expertise,
- details on increase and reduction of capital,
- a directory of charges on the company assets,
- details on the purchase of own shares,
- annual return,
- balance sheet,
- profit and loss account, and
- business report and auditors' report (Triebel, Hodgson, Kellenter 1995, 276).

As formerly mentioned in item 5.4, English companies are also required to conserve the following documents in the registered office, and to keep them available for examination by anybody.

- a directory of the directors and the secretary,
- copies of directors' employment contracts,
- a directory of the shareholders,
- minutes of the annual general meetings,
- a directory of all charges on the company assets,

- copies of all documents which substantiate charges on the company assets that have to be registered, and
- a directory of holders of debentures (Triebel, Hodgson, Kellenter 1995, 276).

Furthermore, a directory of all shares and debentures of the directors, their spouses and minor children in connected companies also has to be maintained. Without having to pay a fee, all company creditors may inspect the business' directories and copies of the company's charges. Additionally, every letter of business correspondence must include the registered firm and seat as well as the location and the number of registration (Triebel, Hodgson, Kellenter 1995, 277).

5.9 Taxation and Insolvency in England

As this paper mainly deals with the administrative seat of the limited in Germany, English taxation and insolvency assumes only a small portion of the paper.

5.9.1 Taxation in England

Dealing with the taxation of an English limited is unproblematic as long as the company's statutory and administrative seats remain in England. In this case, the limited is subject to English tax legislation. The company has to pay corporation tax on profits, whereby the taxable amount consists of capital gains and income profits (Just 2005, 66). The corporation tax return is to be submitted to the responsible Inland Revenue Department.

The entrepreneur sets up the tax return on the basis of his own, independent assessment. It is to be submitted, along with the annual accounts and tax computations, within twelve months after the end of the financial year (Just 2005, 66).

Furthermore, certain revenues of British companies are subject to a withholding tax, which is 20% on interests and 22% on royalties. The value added tax of 17,5% is to be paid to the H.M. Customs & Excise if sales in England have been made, and if these sales have exceeded £58,000 within the last 12 months. The company provides the given VAT registration number of the H.M. Customs & Excise on all invoices (Just 2005, 66).

5.9.2 Insolvency in England

As is the case with taxation, it is also decisive, in the case of insolvency, whether or not the company has, first of all, its centre of activities in England, or, secondly, if it has relocated its administrative seat to Germany.

English law is applied without further problems if the limited's centre of activities is located in England. Most of the English insolvency legislation is contained in the Insolvency Act 1986 (Just 2005, 69).

The Insolvency Act provides for two types of liquidation. The so-called "voluntary winding up" is a liquidation based on a shareholders' decision, while the "compulsory winding up" is liquidation based on judicial order (Schumann 2004, 746).

A winding up of the company, that is mutually agreed to by the shareholders is further separated into two cases, according to English law: a members' voluntary winding up is controlled by the members (shareholders), while a creditors' voluntary winding up is monitored by creditors (Heinz 2004, 27). In both cases, the members deem it impossible to continue running the company because of its liabilities.

Beforehand, however, the managing directors must decide if it is possible to issue a declaration of solvency. This states that, according to the directors, the company is capable of repaying its liabilities within the next 12 months. If the directors do not issue the declaration, or exceed the time limit, the creditors appoint a (official) receiver, and the process is then called creditors' winding up. If the receiver concludes that the company is not capable of meeting its liabilities, though a declaration of solvency has been issued, a creditor's winding up follows in this case, as well. However, if the receiver is convinced that the company will be able to repay the debts, then the proceedings are instead carried on as a members' voluntary winding up (Schumann 2004, 747).

A compulsory winding up takes place if the company is insolvent and if a creditor has applied for such proceedings (Heinz 2004, 27).

A practical alternative to a compulsory winding up by the court is to strike the company off the register. The registrar gives orders to delete a company from the register if he has reason to believe that the company has ceased its business activities for more than a year. In this case, the assets the company may possess fall to the crown (Heinz 2004, 28).

6. The German Branch Office as the Company's Administrative Seat

6.1 The German Branch Office

The globalisation of markets and companies is a common phenomenon, especially within the European Union. Globalization results in an overall internationalisation of trade relations, forming a closely knit global economy, in which products can be manufactured, services may be rendered, and both can be exchanged virtually anywhere. The ability of companies to act internationally thus gains central importance, and the need to be represented locally provokes them to establishment branch offices.

The term branch office is defined in a number of various ways throughout Europe. A major criterion is the branch office's relative degree of autonomy.

In Germany, it is distinguished between dependent business premises, branch offices, and subsidiary companies.

Subsidiary companies of foreign firms are normally established under German law, mostly with a GmbH form of business (Just 2005, 9). However, since the GmbH is not the subject of this paper, this is not studied in detail.

A dependent business premise, on the other hand, is dependent on the main company and subject to its orders. The management is governed from abroad - in this case, from England, where all the decisions and resolutions are recorded, too.

Along with the advantage of a simple registration with (only) the trading standards department and the tax office, several disadvantages also arise. It is impossible to verify the existence through an excerpt of the register. The granting of attorney powers and the separate operation of premises is also not possible (Just 2005, 9).

The main characteristics of an *in*-dependent business premise - or branch office - are spatial, organizational and personal independence (Wachter 2004, 611 (b)). Spatial and organizational independence means that the office contains its own rooms and bank accounts, as well as its own, separate bookkeeping. Personal independence means that the office's manager must be entitled to represent the office in legal relations (Wachter 2004, 611 (b)).

It is imperative for the branch office to be organised in such a manner that it could prevail as a company in its own right if the main office were discontinued (Kögel 2004, 1764). The branch office's activities are required to last a specified amount of time and to resemble those of the main office(Wachter 2004, 611 (b)), i.e. the branch office's activities have to represent a section of the main company's object (Kögel 2004, 1764). It is often the case that the object of foreign companies and that of their domestic branch offices have nothing in common whatsoever. In such cases, the company object is not pursued and, therefore, presumed to be fictional. The question, then, would be whether this object might become the reference for all business activities if the actual business activities are conducted solely by the branch office. Therefore, the company's object, as it is given in the limited's application, is not the decisive factor for the court of register. Instead, the critical factor is the scope of activities of the branch office located in Germany (Kögel 2004, 1764).

Principally speaking, however, there must be an obvious connection between the branch office and the main office. This is either given by a common company core, or by way of a suitable adjunct that states the affiliation (Wachter 2003, 1256).

If the administrative seat in Germany is the company's only seat besides the registered office in England, it cannot be considered a branch office according to Sec. 13d et seq. HGB. Branch offices, in the sense of the HBG, are economically and organisationally independent operating units that are spatially divided from the main office but subject to the main office's control. According to the decisions of the ECJ in the "Centros" (cp. item 4.3) and "Inspire Art" (cp. item 4.5) cases, however, domestic branch and main offices of foreign companies are treated equally. An English limited with its administrative seat in Germany is, therefore, subject to the regulations for domestic branch offices of foreign companies. The branch office may very well be the only place where the company unfolds its business activities, so 'main office' may be the more adequate designation (Heinz 2004, 32).

Further possibilities of utilising a limited in Germany are, for instance, the "Ltd. & Co. KG" and the so-called "Gesellschafter-Limited".

In a "Ltd. & Co. KG" the limited acquires the role of general partner in a German "Kommanditgesellschaft" (Degenhardt 2003, 40). The "KG" is registered. In contrast to other variants, the limited itself does not engage in business. In fact, it is merely the partner with personal liability in a German "Kommanditgesellschaft". The business is done by the "KG" (Süß 2005, 673).

In the "Gesellschafter-Limited" the limited is used as founding partner of a GmbH or an AG. In principle, the legislator requires a capital of € 25,000 when establishing a

GmbH. If there are two persons establishing a GmbH, however, only € 12,500 are required, but the founders are jointly and severally liable for the remainder.
If one of them is unable to pay, the other one is held liable. If there is only one founder, he may utilise a legal entity that takes the place of the second founding partner.
The limited serves this purpose (Degenhardt 2003, 40).

6.2 Registration of the Branch Office

In general, it is recommended that limiteds be registered with German administrative seats as branch offices (independent business premise), for German creditors tend to verify the registration of an English limited prior to concluding a contract with it. The fact that the company has undergone German testing procedures is a signifier of trustworthiness, together with the additional security provided by the public access to documents in Germany and the fact that changes must be reported to the register (Heinz 2004, 32).
German trading law prescribes foreign companies to register their domestic branch offices with the German register, according to the regulations concerning foreign companies in Sec. 13d - 13g and 325a HGB, which are based on the ECJ's directive[4] on branch offices (Ebert, Levedag 2003, 1338). Hence, if a branch office is at issue, there is automatically a duty to register it. Otherwise, the court of register enforces the registration and demands a penalty payment, according to Sec. 14 HGB (Wachter 2003, 1254). However, the registration has no final constitutive effect. Rather, it plays the declaratory role of referring to the establishment abroad (w/o author 2005, 169 (a)). Nevertheless, registration is allowed only if the branch office at issue is a branch office in the spirit of the law. Should any doubts arise, the "Industrie- und Handelskammer" (IHK) is asked for an expertise on this topic, since foreign companies are required to become members of the "IHK", too (Kögel 2004, 1763).
When evaluating the registration status of a foreign company's branch office, German registration law must be followed. For the most part, it depends on the company management's leeway of formation whether a branch office or a mere (dependent) business premise is at issue. This organizational scope does not mean,

---

[4] Eleventh Council Directive 89/666/EEC of 21 December 1989 concerning disclosure requirements in respect of branches opened in a Member State by certain types of company governed by the law of another State.

however, that an organizational unit may instantly be declared a branch office. In order for a branch office to be declared as such, certain requirements must be fulfilled (cp. item 6.1) (Kögel 2004, 1763).

As already mentioned, Sec. 13d – 13g HGB are critical in the registration of a branch office. Sec. 13e subsection 2 HGB lists the duties of the managing director and the documents he must submit for the registration.

Upon registration, the company must prove its existence. Moreover, if governmental permission is required for the company's object or for the allowance to engage in business (as e.g. when plying an independent trade), this acquired approval must also be proven. The registration has to include the full address and the object of the company as well. Furthermore, the register where the company is enlisted must accordingly be stated, along with the entry number. Last but not least, the company's form of business organization must also be named, as well as the persons who are authorized, as permanent representatives for the activities of the company's branch office, to represent the company in and out of court.

A multitude of further regulations are laid down in Sec. 13g HGB. Accordingly, a certified copy of the Articles of Association and - if the articles have not been written in German - a certified translation have to be included.

Special emphasis is also put to the statutory authority of the registering director. A regular shareholder's decision of the director's appointment as authorized representative of the company is required. Minutes of meetings of the board of directors are insufficient (Wachter 2003, 1255). The registration shall, furthermore, include information about the form of business organization, the firm, the seat and the object of the company, as well as, the amount of the company's equity. The concluding date of the Articles of Association, the persons of the managing directors and their power of attorney, and the fixed (or agreed) regulations of the duration are included in the application (Sec. 62 HRV). After the testing, all declarations are entered into the register. The foreign companies are then required to publicise the documents of the main office's accounting in the "Bundesanzeiger", which should already have been submitted to the local register of the branch office (Ebert, Levedag 2003, 1338).

During the examination process of registration prerequisites of the domestic branch offices, the domestic court of register examines the innocuousness of the foreign company's firm according to foreign law, while that of the domestic branch office is analysed according to domestic law.

The following criteria are fixed in German firm law:

- the firm must be true,
- there is no danger of confusion with other firms,
- the firm is recognizable as a foreign company,
- the firm is a branch office,
- the name of the firm and the business form adjunct may be given in a foreign language, as long as they are understandable to the public (Ebert, Levedag 2003, 1338).

In several European Member States virtually every German firm name may be registered. Due to this fact, designations are often encountered regarding the establishment of foreign firms, that would otherwise be considered as misleading under German law, according to Sec. 18 Subsec. 2 HGB (Kögel 2004, 1765).

The domestic branch offices of foreign companies are generally required to state their number of registration, the full foreign firm plus business form adjunct, and the register of the foreign company (Wachter 2003, 1256). However, this information is, in most cases, concealed within the footnotes.

A restriction for such cases is the "ordre public" (Art. 6 EGBGB). Accordingly, the legal norm of another State may not be applied if it functions contrary to fundamental principles of German law. This applies to a foreign company's violations of fundamental principles of German firm law, such as, for example, the use of a misleading company title, or the intentional withholding of the real legal status (Kögel 2004, 1765).

It should be kept in mind that every alteration of the branch office's Articles of Association is to be reported to the court of register. The following is a short list of the factors that should be reported to the court of register: an amendment of the foreign company's Articles of Association, a change in or of the (name of the) firm, changes of the persons who are permanent representatives or in the power of attorney, changes of the persons of the company's managing directors and their power of attorney, the winding up of the company, the receivers of the company and their power of attorney, the institution of bankruptcy (insolvency) proceedings concerning the assets of the company. The court of register should be informed through a fully certified text, submitted along with a translation that defines the facts that have actually changed (Wachter 2003, 1255).

6.3 Permanent Representative

The branch office's application of registration must specify the persons who are authorized to represent the company as a permanent representative for the activities of the branch office (Sec. 13e Subsec. 2 Sent. 4 Clause 3 HGB; Sec. 43 Clause 6 HRV; Sec. 62 Clause 4 Sent. 3 HRV).
The term 'permanent representative' is not legally defined. In the prevailing opinion, the term signifies those persons who, by contractual authorization, are entitled to represent the branch office.
This includes:

- authorized signatories (Sec. 48 et seq. HGB),
- authorized agents, who are entitled to conduct a case (Sec. 54 Subsec. 2 HGB),
- persons with general power of attorney.

It does not include:

- other authorized agents (Sec. 54 Subsec. 1 HGB),
- statutory agents (Wachter 2004, 613 (b)).

Since the representation is permanent the agent's activities should be effective for a certain period of time and not be focused on individual cases. There are a number of different opinions about the duration of this period, varying anywhere from 6 to 12 months.
The name(s) of the permanent representative(s) and the extent of their representative authority have to be included in the registration (cp. item 6.2).
No special legal requirements exist for the person who is appointed permanent representative. Moreover, he is not obliged to certify that there are no impediments

connected to his person that would inhibit him from being appointed (Sec. 8 Subsec. 3 GmbHG).

Nowadays, a person who may not be appointed managing director in Germany (Sec. 6 Subsec. 2 GmbHG), can act as the permanent representative of a domestic branch office (Wachter 2004, 613 (b)).

However, there is no legal obligation to appoint a permanent representative (Sec. 13 Subsec. 4 HGB).

6.4 Liability in the Branch Office

A topic that is heavily being debated, in connection to an English limited based in Germany, are the cases of liability in German law that are applicable to its managing directors and shareholders. In the lifting of the corporate veil (cp. item 5.6), it is exclusively the English law that is applicable. It is an important question, however, in how far certain standards of liability may - or even must - be carried over from German law rather than from the law of the state of association. According to ECJ legislation, regulations that are related to general duties would represent no impediment to the freedom of establishment as long as they would pose no excessive requirements to the respective branch office (Spindler, Berner 2004, 9).

When engaging in domestic business activities, members of the bodies of foreign companies are subject to the same public-law duties (e.g. from taxation law, social security legislation or competition law) as are the bodies of domestic companies. Therefore, they are also held liable personally in breach of duty (Wachter 2003, 1257).

A foreign company must be subjected to the general trading law of the country in which the branch office is located, even if individual facts of the case depict a tendency towards company law.

This includes the law of contract, the law of tort and the insolvency law - as long as they are not used in a discriminating manner. In law of tort, the liability for the commitment of civil offences and for the violation of third-party rights by fault, respectively, depends on the location of the respective act of tort, according to Art. 40 EGBGB, and not on company law (Horn 2004, 899).

The individual Member states generally have the jurisdiction concerning the criminal law. However, the German penal provisions must not result in a discrimination or in an impediment to the basic freedoms guaranteed by Community law, since Community law possesses priority over domestic criminal law (Spindler, Berner 2004, 14).

The following chapter discusses, in detail, the extent to which the German-law measures of "Kapitalerhaltungshaftung", "Existenzvernichtungshaftung", and "Insolvenzverschleppungshaftung" are applicable to English limiteds with a German branch office.

6.4.1 "Kapitalerhaltungshaftung"

"Kapitalerhaltungshaftung" [capital conservation liability] is regulated in Sec. 30, 31 GmbHG for the German GmbH. Accordingly, the company's assets that are required for the conservation of the equity capital may not be paid out to the shareholders. The question of whether or not the creditor protection regulations of "Kapitalerhaltungshaftung" also apply to the limited that has its administrative seat in Germany, seems to be a relatively difficult one. An application is, partly, rejected by scholars, on the basis that most foreign company laws rely on their own concepts for creditor protection. Additionally, Sec. 30, 31 GmbHG are tailored on the German GmbH business organization form. Therefore, they are inappropriate for the English limited (w/o author 2005, 151 (b)).

This interpretation, however, which has also not been clearly manifested in ECJ legislation yet, is precarious in the light of legislation policy, for the only factor upon which a possible creditor may rely on when contemplating the question of whether or not their protection is guaranteed, is the foreign firm name.

Therefore, it does not go against the freedom of establishment if foreign companies are denied the right to distribute subscribed capital in Germany (w/o author 2005, 151 (b)).

In this, a mere refund of equity capital to shareholders who would reimburse their GmbH in case of insolvency is, technically speaking, only of minor importance. On the contrary, a bigger issue is payments that are detrimental to the assets covering outside capital. This would result in a still bigger over-indebtedness.

As a result, legal relations are considerably endangered. This, in turn, is detrimental to creditors, too, and leads to over-indebtedness, as well. Therefore, Sec. 30, 31 GmbHG must be applicable to companies operating in Germany (w/o author 2005, 151 (b)).

Meilicke, for instance, claims that a German judge may not apply German "Kapitalersatzrecht" [law on capital substitution] when treating limiteds having their administrative seat in Germany. Instead, the judge must search for any comparable regulations of the state of association (cp. item 5.5.2) (Meilicke 2003, 1272).

A concluding decision on the matter is yet to be reached by the ECJ.

6.4.2 "Existenzvernichtungshaftung"

The protection objective of "Existenzvernichtungshaftung" [liability in case of destruction of existence] is similar to that of "Kapitalerhaltungshaftung". The BGH developed the legal instrument of "Existenzvernichtungshaftung" in 2001, in order to improve the creditor's security. The company's creditors are given a direct claim against the shareholder who drives his company into insolvency by withdrawing the assets necessary for setting its liabilities from the company (Meilicke 2003, 1272). The BGH characterizes the "Existenzvernichtungshaftung" as a liability that belongs to company law and clearly differentiates it from liability for civil offences, such as, for example, a premeditated unethical damaging of creditors in the spirit of Sec. 826 BGB (Altmeppen 2004, 101).

Altmeppen considers the application of "Existenzvernichtungshaftung" on a limited having its administrative seat in Germany as justified, since the destruction of assets, which are mandatory for the creditors' satisfaction, through the actions of the shareholders and managing directors, would result in the breach of an elementary principle of creditor protection (Altmeppen 2004, 101). Wachter, too, considers a personal liability of the shareholders of limiteds having their administrative seat in Germany to be appropriate in the case of action that is destructive to the existence, provided that the shareholders had not paid adequate attention to the company's interests, which then resulted in damage to the company's creditors (Wachter 2003, 1257).

According to Schumann, however, the German concept of "Existenzvernichtungshaftung" is tailored on the GmbH. It is neither part of insolvency law, nor of the law of tort, but instead, of company law. In his opinion, an enforcement of liability on shareholders should, therefore, principally follow English law (Schumann 2004, 749).

However, there is more to this subject and future developments in legislation are to be expected.

6.4.3 "Insolvenzantragspflicht" and "Insolvenzverschleppungshaftung"

A cornerstone of German creditor protection is Sec. 64 Subsec. 1 GmbHG, which obliges the managing director to immediately file for insolvency in case of over-indebtedness or insolvency of the company (w/o author 2005, 215 (b)).

A managing director of a GmbH would commit a criminal offence if he delays in, or even fails to file for insolvency, according to Sec. 84 Subsec. 1 Clause 2 GmbHG, and in conjunction with Sec. 823 Subsec. 2 BGB he is personally held liable to the creditors.

The question however is, which law is applicable for a limited having its administrative seat in Germany, concerning the "Insolvenzantragspflicht" [duty to file for insolvency] and the "Insolvenzverschleppungshaftung" [liability due to obstruction of insolvency].

Again, there are differing opinions on the matter. Since the "Insolvenzantragspflicht" is regulated in German company law, while the limited possesses an English company statute, the application of German legal standards that call for insolvency proceedings is partly rejected. English law would be the only law to be applied in this case.

Any commitment or obligation to file for insolvency would then be secured by the managing director's liability due to "wrongful trading" and "fraudulent trading" (cp. item 5.6). These English legal standards include, at least up to a certain amount, the German measures, but are no equivalent thereof. Some scholars describe them as a component of company law, as well. Therefore, a probable duty to file for insolvency, as well as a possible liability due to obstruction of insolvency, should be solely designated to English law (Just 2005, 75).

Secondly, Schumann professed that he would direct such a duty to file for insolvency to company law, i.e. to English law, since it corresponds to the managing director's duty to act in a certain economic situation (Schumann 2004, 746).

Riedemann and Wachter oppose this view. According to Sec. 64 Subsec. 1 GmbHG, the "Insolvenzantragspflicht" is to be addressed as an element of insolvency law, regardless of its original status in company law, since, according to Sec. 15 InsO, the law of "Insolvenzantragspflicht" is seen as a constituent of insolvency law. Furthermore, there is a close connection of the *right to file* and the *duty to file* for insolvency (Riedemann 2004, 348). As a result, the "Insolvenzantragspflicht" is also to be applied to the managing bodies of foreign limited liability companies that have their administrative seat in Germany (Wachter 2004, 101 (a)).

Yet, Riedemann does not perceive this duty to be an impediment to the freedom of establishment, since it is a measure resulting from mandatory reasons of public interest - in this case creditor protection - and since it is appropriate for this aim. The "Insolvenzantragspflicht" is, therefore, deemed a justified restriction (Riedemann 2004, 348).

Again, one has to keep in mind that the legal position in questions of the "Insolvenzantragspflicht" and the "Insolvenzverschleppungshaftung" still remains largely unclear. At the moment, a common, uniform regulation of such a liability, due to obstruction of insolvency, is being discussed on a European level.

6.5 "Mitbestimmung"

The German laws of "Mitbestimmung"[5] [workers' co-determination] have been heavily under discussion. The question is whether or not they are applicable to the English limited having its administrative seat in Germany. The danger, or the chances, of circumventing the German "Mitbestimmung" law is one of the fascinating facets of the English limited and might as well be an important motive in the decision for this form of business organization. Legal regulations of the workers' "Mitbestimmung" are widely familiar to companies with limited liability outside of Germany. However, in Germany the regulations of the "Mitbestimmung" law are applied only to companies which employ more than 2000 people. "Mitbestimmung" of workers' representatives in companies employing at least 500, but less than 2000 people, is asserted in the "Drittelbeteiligungsgesetz" (Second law for facilitation of the election of workers' representatives to the non-executive board, 5.18.2004 BGBl). These companies have a board of non-executive directors that is split in three

---

[5] "Mitbestimmung" means a participation of workers in the decisions of the company's bodies.

parities. The "Mitbestimmung" law is not applied in GmbHs with less than 500 employees (Wachter 2005, 730).

"Mitbestimmung" is to be seen as a part of the company statutes, according to Bayer. Therefore it has to be attributed to the Articles of Association. An application of the German "Mitbestimmung" on a limited established in England would thus be an intervention into the foreign organizational statute and an impediment to the freedom of establishment that is unjustifiable through the means of a decisive domestic public interest (Bayer 2004, 4). Kallmeyer also believes that the "Mitbestimmung" law is not applicable to limiteds with administrative seat within Germany, since it would require the limited to have an obligatory board of non-executive directors and would thus intervene in the English company statute (Kallmeyer 2004, 638). Wachter supports this view, proclaiming that the use of the "Mitbestimmung" law - as an abstract regulation - is not directed against the unjustified use of the freedom of establishment in a concrete isolated instance. Therefore, it represents an unjustified impediment of the European freedom of establishment (Wachter 2004, 92 (a)).

Von Halen gathers that workers' "Mitbestimmung" is one of the most fundamental principles of German law, making it "ordre public" (cp. item 6.2), which leads to the application of German law (von Halen 2003, 571).

Riegger, on the other hand, remarks that this interpretation is actually not convincing in the light of the differentiation of the German workers' "Mitbestimmung", since it is not applicable to companies with less than 500 employees. According to his view, worker's "Mitbestimmung" is not significant enough to be applied to all companies. Therefore, one could not speak of an "ordre public"(Riegger 2004, 510).

In most cases, the question of "Mitbestimmung" is not a problem, since the majority of German GmbHs and limiteds having their administrative seat in Germany employ far less than 500 workers (Wachter 2005, 730).

6.6 Transfer of Shares in the Branch Office

Since the transfer of shares is an internal procedure of the company, it is exclusively regulated by English law. The transfer of shares has already been treated in item 5.7 and is therefore not treated in detail here.

6.7 Accounting, Audit and Disclosure in the Branch Office

According to Sec. 264 Subsec. 2 HGB, a German company's annual accounts have to relate an adequate impression of the financial status and income situation, in compliance with the generally accepted accounting principles (GAAP).

Since accounting principles are usually considered to be inherent in company law, no necessity for a recourse to German legal norms exists. Specific connections to German accounting regulations would go against the freedom of establishment. Of course, these connections would only be justified if the application of German accounting regulations was demanded because of creditor protection issues. The protection, however, is already guaranteed by the English accounting regulations (cp. item 5.8.1) (Just 2005, 60).

Even if accounting regulations were to be considered public-law, the accounting for the limited having its administrative seat in Germany would, nevertheless, still have to proceed according to English law, as directed in Sec. 325a HGB in conjunction with Art. 3 of the 'directive on disclosure' (council directive 68/151/EEC).

According to Sec. 325a Subsec. 1 HGB, the accounting documents of the main office, which have been drawn up, audited and disclosed according to the law that is relevant for that office, have to be made available. The respective law for the main office, in turn, is determined by Art. 3 of the directive on disclosure. Accordingly, the duty of disclosure includes only those accounting documents which have been drawn up under the law of the Member State to which the company is subject to. The law of the statutory seat, which is English law, is therefore decisive (cp. item 5.8.3) (Riegger 2004, 510).

All necessary documents must be submitted in German to the register of the branch office's seat. Since the official language of the main office of an English limited based in Germany is, however, not German, the documents may either be submitted in English or in a certified copy retrieved from the main office's register. In this case, a certified translation of the register's certification into German has to be attached, according to Sec. 325a HGB (Wachter 2004, 617 (b)).

Besides this, the statutory audit and the audit of the annual accounts are also determined exclusively by English law (cp. item 5.8.2). This results from the fact that there is no obligation to draw up any domestic annual accounts. If the accounts are missing, there is, naturally, no object for a domestic audit under Sec. 316 et seq. HGB (Just 2005, 63).

6.8 Taxation of the Branch Office in Germany

6.8.1 Taxation on the Limited's Level

As formerly mentioned in item 5.9.1, the taxation of the limited depends on the location of its head office or of its administrative seat - that is, the location where the company engages in business activities. If the limited has relocated its administrative seat to Germany in order to do its operative business there, it is subject to taxation only there (Heinz 2004, 20).

In other words, this means that the limited has to pay taxes on its entire, worldwide income specifically in Germany.

Generally, in Germany there is no difference between the taxation of the profits of an Ltd. and a GmbH.

The tax-related treatment of English limiteds with German-situated branch office is regulated in the double taxation agreement (DTA) between Germany and Great Britain[6]. According to Art. 3 of the DTA the company's profits are taxable under the law of the state where they have been realized if they can clearly be attributed to a business premise that is located there. The income is then taxed exclusively in Germany on grounds of the DTA while it is accordingly exempted from tax in England.

A company is subject to unlimited taxability in Germany if either its head office or management is located there (Sec. 1 Subs. 1 KStG). The management is, according to Sec. 10 AO, the centre of the business administration and is conducted from the location where the relevant intent of the management is formed. The location of the company's seat is, according to Sec. 11 AO, determined either by law, by the memorandum and / or the Articles of Association, or other such sources.

Even if management is conducted from England, the limited may still be subject to German tax law if engaging in business activities by way of a business premise (branch office, production plant, branch agency) located in Germany (Art. III DTA with UK). If a business premise in Germany exists, the limited is subject to taxation in both countries. Concerning the world-wide sales and profits of the German business premise, though the company would be unlimitedly taxable in GB, it would

---

[6] Convention of 26 November 1964 between the FRG and UK for the Avoidance of Double Taxation and the Prevention of Fiscal Evasion / as amended by the Protocol of 23 March 1971, BStBl. 1971 I, Sent. 139, BGBl. 1971 II Sent. 45.

be limitedly taxable in Germany (Just 2005, 67). If no taxable income has been realized in England, the limited is nevertheless required to submit a tax return at the registered office's location there, even though this might be a zero tax declaration, and regardless of the yearly tax return submitted in Germany (Happ, Holler 2004, 736).

If German tax law is applied to the English limited, corporation tax (including the "Solidaritätszuschlag" (solidarity surcharge) for the former East-German countries), (local) business tax and value added tax (on sales in Germany) will be payable according to German tax law (Korts 2004, 52). The corporation tax rate is 25% at the moment, while the "Solidaritätszuschlag" amounts to 5,5 % (Sec. 1 Subsec. 2 KStG in conjunction with Sec. 23 Subsec. 1 KStG). It is imposed if a positive amount of the tax base, i.e. of the determined corporation tax, remains.

Through its qualification as a stock company, the limited is, much like the GmbH, subject to (local) business tax by provision of Sec. 2 Subsec. 2 GewStG. The business tax may amount to up to 19,68 % of taxable profits, depending on the community's tax rate, in which the limited holds its business in. The allowance of € 24,500 according to Sec. 11 Subsec. 1 Sent. 3 Clause. 1 GewStG, as well as the graduated tariff, which is granted to persons and partnerships, according to Sec. 11 Subsec. 2 Clause 1 GewStG, is not applicable to the limited as a stock company.

The regular value added tax rate is 16 %, while the reduced rate is 7 %. It is to be paid on the taxable sales according to Sec. 1 UStG (Sec. 12 UStG).

After the deduction of input tax any remaining pay charges must be remitted to the tax office.

However, while the tax bureau of the community where the branch office is located is responsible for the income taxes, the area of foreign companies' value-added tax is assigned to a central tax office depending on the respective country. The tax bureau "Hannover Nord" is responsible for English companies (Sec. 21 AO).

6.8.2 Taxation on the Shareholder's Level

6.8.2.1 The Limited's Distribution of Profits to Shareholders

If the limited distributes profits to a shareholder, this payment is subject to investment income tax of 20% of the distributed profits (Sec. 43 Subsec. 1 Clause 1,

Sec. 43a Subsec. 1 Clause 1 EStG). The limited withholds the amount and remits it to the responsible tax office.

If the shareholder is a domestic resident, half of the distribution of profits is subject to income tax, according to the so-called semi-income-system (Sec. 3 Clause 40, Sec. 3c Subsec. 2 EStG). The withheld investment income tax is then deducted from the income tax.

A shareholder resident in Great Britain is principally subject to German taxation regarding the profits distributed to him (Sec. 9 Subsec. 1 Clause. 5a EStG). In Germany, investment income tax is levied (Sec. 43 Subsec. 1 Clause 1 EStG). According to the DTA, this must not exceed 15% between the FRG and GB 15 %, provided that the distribution of profits is taxable in GB (Art. 6 Subsec. 1 DTA GB) (Höreth, Schiegl 2004, 11).

6.8.2.2 Sale of Shares in the Limited

If a shareholder sells shares in the limited, the taxation also depends on the domestic or foreign status of the shareholder.

A domestic shareholder has to subject half of the sale's profits to income tax (Sec 3 Clause 40, Sec 3c Subsec. 2 EStG). Additionally, the solidarity surcharge of 5,5 % of the income tax has to be disbursed (Sec 1 Subsec. 1, Sec. 3 Subsec. 1 Clause 1 SolZG).

The profits a shareholder, who is a resident of Great Britain, realizes in the sale are on principle subject to limited taxability in Germany (Sec. 49 Subsec. 1 Clause. 2e EStG); however, as far as GB is concerned in the DTA, it is stipulated that these profits may be taxed exclusively in GB (Art. 8 Subsec. 3 DTA GB). Accordingly, no tax is to be paid in Germany (Höreth, Schiegl 2004, 11).

6.9 Insolvency of the Branch Office in Germany

The insolvency process regarding an English limited with an administrative seat in Germany is complicated and oftentimes legally dubious. However, along with the number of relocations of these businesses to Germany, the number of insolvent English stock companies should increase as well. If, and under which circumstances the shareholders and members of bodies are personally liable for debts of the foreign company, in the case of an insolvency, generally depends on the Articles of Association. Thus, in a limited, it depends on English company law, regardless of the administrative seat (cp. item 5.6) (Schumann 2004, 745).

However, liability of the shareholders and body members is not ruled out under the regulations of the German contract and criminal law (cp. item 6.4).

At the time being, the question of which insolvency law should be applied to companies from a foreign EU-country and, additionally, which jurisdiction is responsible for conducting the insolvency proceedings, is heavily controversial. This question requires, first of all, the consultation of the European Council Regulation on Insolvency Proceedings (EuInsVO).

According to Art. 3 Subsec. 1 Sent. 1 EuInsVO the courts of the Member state in which the creditor's centre of main interests is located are responsible for the institution of the main insolvency proceedings. The place where the creditor normally conducts his administrative activities is called the "centre of main interests" (Riedemann 2004, 347). According to Article 3 Subsec. 1 Sent. 2 EuInsVO, the "centre of main interests" of a company or legal entity is supposed to be located at its statutory seat. This can, however, be refuted, since there is a disintegration of the statutory and administrative seat in companies that do not engage in any business in their state of association. This is especially significant to a limited whose domicile is in Germany. In such cases the administrative seat is generally considered to be the "centre of main interests" (Schumann 2004, 746).

According to Art. 4 Subsec. 1 EuInsVO, the insolvency law of the Member State in which the proceedings have been instituted also applies (lex fori concursus) (Pannen, Riedemann 2005, 497). This law regulates the factors under which insolvency proceedings will be instituted and determines how these proceedings are conducted and completed.

An English limited that has its administrative seat in Germany is therefore subject to German insolvency law before a German court, i.e. before the court of the seat's location.

Besides over-indebtedness or actual insolvency of the company, the threat of an insolvency might also be a reason for the institution of insolvency proceedings, provided that a creditor has filed for the institution of such proceedings (Sec. 18 InsO).

The right to file for insolvency must be considered as belonging to insolvency law, and, therefore, it is regulated by German law. According to this, every member that is authorized to represent the company is entitled the right to file for insolvency. On the other hand, the English law regulates the authorization of persons who may represent the company, according to the Articles of Association (Pannen, Riedemann 2005, 498).

Yet an even more complicated matter is the question of which law is applicable for the "Insolvenzantragspflicht" [duty to file for insolvency] and the "Insolvenzverschleppungshaftung" [liability due to obstruction of insolvency]. Since the topic has already been discussed in item 6.4.3, there is no need for further speculation here.

Another problem is how to qualify the concept of equitable subordination [Eigenkapitalersatzregeln][7] in insolvency law.

According to German insolvency law, the refund of capital-replacing loans may be appealed if the refund was placed during the last year before filing for insolvency (Sec. 135 Clause 2 InsO). The appeal relates explicitly to the insolvency statute passed by the European Council Regulation on Insolvency Proceedings. This means that German law is applied to the appeal (Art. 4 Subsec. 2 Sent. EuInsVO).

However, another question is whether or not the standards of German law are applicable in determining if a capital-replacing loan is at issue. According to Just however, the capitalisation requirements unequivocally belong to company statute, or, in other words, to English law (Just 2005, 76). Pannen and Riedemann claim that after the ECJ's decision in the "Inspire Art"-case (cp. item 4.5), it seems out of the question for the ECJ to allow a measuring of capitalisation requirements in which the host state's rules of equitable subordination are applied (Pannen, Riedemann 2005, 498).

The conduction and conclusion of the insolvency proceedings depend on the law of that state in which the proceedings are instituted (Art. 4 Subsec. 2 Sent. 1 EuInsVO). The administration and disposal rights of the limited's assets are conferred to the German receiver through the opening of bankruptcy proceedings (Sec. 80 InsO). The single authorizations of the receiver follow the insolvency statute (Riedemann 2004, 349).

---

[7] Directors must prevent payments to shareholders when the money is needed to preserve the nominal share capital in the case of an insolvency.

Among other things, the German insolvency law regulates which assets belong to the legal estate, the distribution of returns, and the conclusion of proceedings. It also specifies the prerequisites under which claims may be filed (Pannen, Riedemann 2005, 498).

However, insolvency procedures for foreign companies with administrative seats in Germany remain unclarified and are controversial in many aspects. According to the latest ECJ jurisdiction, this is because company and insolvency statute disintegrate in such insolvency cases (Pannen, Riedemann 2005, 497). Special national and international legislation concerning such cases will most likely be implemented as soon as relevant instances arise.

7. Perspectives and Risks of Establishing a Limited in Germany

7.1 Advantages of the Limited Compared to the GmbH

The advantages of the limited are evident in its faster, easier, and cheaper process of establishment and the lack of a minimum share capital. Additionally, shareholders receive aid in raising capital and transferring shares. "Mitbestimmung" also is not common in English law and, consequentially, does not apply to the limited. This significantly facilitates the management of such a company. Furthermore, employees and other members of a limited are protected against liability and shareholders may disclose their decisions without the need of notarial authentification.

Small and medium-sized businesses place particular significance on the duration and costs of an establishment when determining the form of business organization (Happ, Holler 2004, 734).

"Normal service" establishment costs about £20 and is obtained within one week, while an express-establishment takes about 24 hours and costs an additional £60. The two to three months establishment time of a GmbH is relatively long in comparison to that of a limited (Bartsch 2005, 1).

Lately, a host of service enterprises have appeared that take charge of the establishing formalities of a limited. These companies provide for a secretary, registered office, and are available for further legal advice. However, prices are clearly different and range from € 250 to € 1,200 (Werner 2004, 51).

Another eminent advantage of the limited, in comparison to the GmbH, involves the regulations on capital raising. They are namely less severe. A mandatory minimum share capital of € 25,000, half of which must be offered as downpayment, is unknown to English company law. Additionally, services, besides deposits and non-cash contributions, may be contributed without closer inspection (cp. item 5.5.1).

The risk of a covered non-cash contribution that founders of businesses face when furnishing the company with capital contribution does not accrue to the limited, as neither do special regulations concerning shareholder loans that replace equity [kapitalersetzenden Gesellschafterdarlehen] (Kallmeyer 2004, 636).

It is still not clear how far the German law of "Mitbestimmung" is to be applied to a limited resident in Germany. It may be expected, however, that it is not applicable to limiteds (cp. item 6.5.). This would point to another advantage of the limited over the GmbH.

Furthermore, it is advantageous to the limited's shareholders that issues internal to the company are dependent only on shareholders' decisions, which do not require notarial authentification, as would be the case with the German GmbH (Kallmeyer 2004, 638).

The written form, along with the additional entry in the register, is sufficient even for the transfer of shares (cp. item 6.6). Since the consultation of a notary is required neither in the transfer of shares, nor in other shareholder's decisions, the limited incurs far less costs than the GmbH.

In comparison to shareholders of a GmbH, shareholders of the limited benefit from a better protection of their private fortunes (cp. item 6.4). Liability enforcements in an English limited take place only under the provisions of English law, provided that the prerequisites of a civil offence, which would result in liability according to German law, are not at issue.

The reputation of the limited, being the world's most renown form of business organization, may be advantageous for "German" limiteds that are doing, or plan to do, business on an international basis.

The GmbH form of business organization on the other hand, is rather unfamiliar, and may, thus, be disadvantageous, because it may repel possible business partners (Werner 2004, 51).

Companies seeking to move single operational hazards out of their business fields can do so by establishing a limited. The limited then covers its proper business segment and is separated from the mother company. However, a consultation over tax issues is recommendable in each case.

As previously mentioned in item 6.1, the limited may assume the general partner's function in a German "Kommanditgesellschaft". In Germany, it is therefore possible to use the limited form of business organization, as well as the "Limited & Co. KG" form. This variant of the "Kommanditgesellschaft" allows for the combination of the respective advantages of both limited and partnership.

In this form of business organization, the limited assumes the role of the personally liable general partner, so that the limited's liability is more or less restricted to its investment. The main reason or advantage in choosing a limited over a GmbH is that limited partners search for a general partner who is cheap in terms of capital endowment. However, there is another advantage that is often overseen. According to Art. 11 Subs. 3 of the Anglo-German double taxation agreement, one has the choice to decide whether the taxation of the directors' remuneration should take place in Great Britain, or in Germany. Under this provision, directors whose residency is located in Germany can evade the domestic Treasury and appreciate the lower income taxes in Britain, which is, thus, the only country to which they pay taxes. However, they would then lose German tax deductions such as personal allowances (Heinz 2004, 31).

Nonetheless, it is not only the founders of a limited that are at an advantage, but also any business partners, investors and creditors. Benefits include the improved conservation of capital (cp. item 5.5.2) and the increased transparency that is common with enlarged duties of disclosure (cp. item 5.8.3).

7.2 Disadvantages and Risks of the Limited Compared to the GmbH

The limited's disadvantages, in comparison to the GmbH, lie in the language barrier and in legal advice that is clearly harder to obtain. At the moment, the limited still misses acceptance and reputation in general German business and legal practice. The unaccustomed handling with legal institutions such as the registered office and the company secretary is a further difficulty. The current costs, which among other things include the registered office's maintenance costs and the company secretary's salary, should not be underestimated as well. Further disadvantages and complications also arise in the legal uncertainty of the limited, due to various issues that yet remain unsolved, and in the overlapping of the legal systems (as e.g. in insolvency-, tax- and liability law), which diminishes planning reliability and liability protection. Besides this, the work- and cost-intensive procedure of registering the limited in the German register is another factor of inconvenience.

7.2.1 Current Costs

Many Internet-ventures that specialize in the establishment of limited companies, spark up the interest of potential business owners by highlighting the low costs of establishment. The existing costs that befall during the administration process are scarcely mentioned, if at all. However, these costs are vital and should be included in the calculations, as they should not be underestimated. Further expenses accrue from the establishment and maintenance of the registered office (cp. item 5.4) and the secretary's salary – provided that secretary duties are assumed by an independent third person (cp. item 5.3.3). In addition, expenses also cover the reporting and disclosure duties (cp. item 5.8) to which the business is obligated to, in accordance with English company law.

Furthermore, the registration of the branch office in Germany and the respective updates to the German register must be taken into account, since they also require a considerable amount of time and money (Happ, Holler 2004, 735).

Due to this disintegration of statutory and actual seat, a problem results from the fact that all legal issues concerning the limited adhere to English law. The following are a few examples: when to take what resolutions, how the company should be represented, under what circumstances a managing director violates the restraint of trade, under what circumstances one of the partners might be excluded from the company, which compensation has to be paid, and when liability occurs, due to a breach of duty. These questions can only be answered with the help of expensive, English legal advice (Maul, Schmidt 2003, 2298).

A small company may thus incur extra-costs (litigation under English law, consultation of multiple, internationally experienced lawyers etc.) on a regular basis during its existence.

However, access to English legal advice is rather scarce in Germany and if obtainable, in economic centres such as Frankfurt, Hamburg, Munich or Berlin. It is nevertheless ineffective, as it does not cover the whole area.

The costs of the tax consultation also leads to higher expenses for an English limited situated in Germany, since two tax returns, one for Germany and one for Great Britain, respectively, have to be completed and submitted (cp. item 6.8).

Even if the English language is omnipresent in German business life, there is, nevertheless, a language barrier. The fact that the entire company document is written in English is a considerable disadvantage. The legal terminology of the Articles of Association or the Memorandum of Association is hard to understand for those with no special knowledge of judicial English, regardless of how good their English is otherwise. An expensive translator or interpreter is therefore necessary.

According to a study conducted by a market survey institute, the current costs amount to about € 800 per year (Bartsch 2005, 1).

7.2.2 Legal Uncertainty

Since the ECJ's decisions in "Centros", "Überseering" and "Inspire Art", the European company law allows the freedom to choose which country's law is to be applied. There is also a significant amount of legal uncertainty in Germany regarding the applicable law of foreign companies whose residency is located in Germany. There is an overwhelming concern about the application of German company law in so far as these companies are involved. On the grounds of the "Inspire Art" decision (cp. item 4.5), the company law of a single Member State is applicable, as are the company laws of other Member States, for their companies may establish their administrative seat in every other state as well. German judges and lawyers are therefore compelled not only to master the full extent of the German and English company laws, but also to study the company laws of all the 25 Member States in order to be able to apply them in litigation concerning the German branch office (Altmeppen 2004, 98).

According to Dierksmeier, the possibility that the courts will have to turn to consultants will then increase. This, in turn, considerably increases current costs and expenses for expectable litigations (cp. item 7.2.1) (Dierksmeier 2005, 1522).

As explained in item 6.4, "liability in the branch office", in connection with the subordinated items of "Kapitalerhaltungshaftung", "Existenzvernichtungshaftung", "Insolvenzantrags-pflicht", and "Insolvenzverschleppungshaftung", commentary expresses several, clearly contrasting opinions regarding the application of the respective legal system in the individual areas of application.

Even in connection to the German concepts of liability in creditor protection, there is heated debate, as many views are in conflict with each other.

In the ruling of "Inspire Art", the ECJ has emphasized the fact that creditor protection is a specific protective good in the spirit of the general interest. It is still unclear however, in how far it will be possible to apply the German creditor protection law for foreign companies having its administrative seat in Germany.

According to the ECJ's jurisdiction, mandatory reasons of public interest, as for example the protection of creditors' interest, would justify, under certain circumstances and in compliance with certain requirements, a restriction of the freedom of establishment and, thus, a possible applicability of the German creditor protection law for foreign companies having its administrative seat in Germany. The

ECJ declares that a restriction of the freedom of establishment may be justified only by the "four-criteria-test" or the "Gebhardt-Formula" (cp. item 4.3).

However, the question of which national measures would pass this test is debatable at the present time (Dierksmeier 2005, 1519).

It should be expected that certain individual overrulings over the foreign company statute will be acknowledged, although these would have to be justified with the "Gebhardt-Formula" (Dierksmeier 2005, 1519).

Likewise, it has not yet been clarified whether a mandatory membership of a foreign corporation (like the limited) in the "Industrie- und Handelskammer" (IHK) is a violation of the freedom of establishment (Just 2005, 12). However, the prevailing opinion is that a limited that has its administrative seat in Germany is still subject to general German laws and, thus, also subject to the duty of paying membership dues to the local "IHK" (Heinz 2004, 30/ Wachter 2004, 98 (a)).

Presumably, there is some kind of agreement that the law of the state of association is exclusively applicable for fundamental decisions like amendments to the company's Articles of Association, resolutions of the company's bodies, the conversion of the company, or the question at what time the company is deemed extinct. German courts are not responsible in these cases (Altmeppen 2004, 98).

As long as there is no uniform European law, especially in the area of company law, there will be overlappings of the single legal systems, as an exact determination of applicable law is, generally speaking, impossible.

The developments and decisions of the ECJ on this matter will last a while still. In the meantime, we can count on legal uncertainty well into the future. This will be a great disadvantage for founders of limiteds.

7.2.3 Creditworthiness

Sceptics of the limited argue that a limited's creditworthiness is smaller than that of a German GmbH. This is true, insofar as banks consider equity and profit prospects as crucial for the attainment of a credit. Of course, a limited that has an equity of one or one-hundred pounds is somewhat in a disadvantage if compared to the GmbH with its € 25,000. In the end, however, these € 25,000 are merely considered a bona fide limit (Happ, Holler 2004, 732).

It is irrelevant to a bank whether the company possesses an equity of € 25,000 or not. In both cases, either the bank or the creditor will search for adequate securities, such as, for instance, a guarantee by the shareholders. In the limited, this is due to the missing equity, while in a GmbH it is because the equity is not at all secure (Heinz 2004, 21).

When it comes to credit allocation, it is, rather, the company's profit prospects that are most important of all (Kallmeyer 2004, 637).

If everything with the business plan and securities is in tact, then there should be no further hindrance to the allocation of a credit.

However, the provision of additional securities results in further costs to the shareholders and raises the limitation of liability of companies with limited liability considerably (Wachter 2004, 92 (a)).

In other words, it is due to the financing practice of the capital providers concerning creditworthiness that a limited does not have considerable disadvantages compared to the GmbH in Germany.

Dierksmeier, on the other hand, believes that without a bigger equity base, access to debt capital will be more difficult for the limited than for the GmbH, since, according to German law of property, there is no possibility for issuing debentures. In England, these debentures are secured by a so-called floating charge. This is a typical means of securitization in English law, which 'floats' on the company assets. It charges the entire assets of the company, regardless of what assets belong to it at the respective point in time. This way of securitization is the cornerstone of debt capital access for limiteds in England (Dierksmeier 2005, 1521).

7.2.4 The German Register of Companies

The German company register has a long tradition. It has always kept resisting reforms and adaptations to technological processes and economic developments (Gernoth 2004, 837). At the moment, therefore, it is out-of-date in comparison to most other countries in Europe (Gernoth 2004, 841). It is incomprehensible to foreign business partners why it is that German subsidiaries must wait weeks before finally being registered, because of tedious, formal requirements, which have not been fulfilled yet (Kögel 2003, 1225).

As far as the process of converting the register to electronic storage (digitalization) is concerned, Germany is, unlike other EU countries, not technically up-to-date.

Furthermore, the reform of the directive on disclosure has resulted in the requirement that the Member States must sustain their registers electronically from 2007 onwards (Gernoth 2004, 837). The definition of branch office has also been outdated, as it has been in use ever since the "Reichsgericht". Several of its criteria have been questionable for some time, especially since the reform of the HGB in 1998. At that time, the register of companies was made accessible for very small business traders, as well. Hence, a commercial business whose company may not represent a business trade but whose firm is registered, is deemed as an optionally registrable trader ("Kannkaufmann")[8]. According to Sec 2 HGB, the entrepreneur may be entitled to execute the registration. However, he is not required to do so. Even in the case of a voluntary registration, the establishment is not inspected. As a result, practically stricter regulations apply to the branch office than to any other given main office (Kögel 2004, 1765). In this context, Kallmeyer, professes the registration of a branch office to be more complicated than the establishment of a German GmbH as subsidiary of the English Ltd.. Therefore, the limited with administrative seat in Germany does not inhibit an advantage with regard to registration in the German company register (Kallmeyer 2004, 637).

A constant problematic issue is the fact that the branch office must – at least partly – engage in the same business area(s) as the main office. This registration requirement does not satisfy the economy's needs (Kögel 2004, 1765).

Even if a limited has been legally established in England, this does not mean that the German courts of register will register the branch office. Some courts of register deny registration of limited companies in individual cases, in spite of the recognition of legal capacity of companies that have been established abroad by the "Bundesgerichtshof" [Federal Court of Justice]. For instance the register of Berlin-Charlottenburg denies registration of a limited if its directors or shareholders are obviously without means. In this, the court presumes that a person who has been registered in the directory of debtors after having made a statutory declaration, does not have the financial means to furnish the company with the necessary capital.

---

[8] An optionally registrable ("Kannkaufmann") trader is someone who runs a commercial business that does not have the required scope to automatically make him a trader. According to Sec. 2 HGB, an optionally registrable trader is free to choose if he wants to get registered or not. If he does, he is treated as a trader.

Therefore, after an insolvency, there is oftentimes no possibility to economically start over in Germany by establishing a limited (Bauhoff 2004, 830).

Founders of limiteds may be shocked when the mandatory publishing of the registration is due. While in a GmbH a downpayment of € 150 to € 200 is the norm, the publishing of a limited's entry in the German register of companies may sometimes even cost up to € 3000. This is due to the excessively detailed description of a limited's company object under English law. Accordingly, the costs of the texts that are to be published in the "Bundesanzeiger" [German Federal Gazette] or in the daily newspaper are also relatively high (Bauhoff 2004, 828). This, in turn, dramatically raises expenses (cp. item 7.2.1).

Gernoth calls for an improved cost-efficiency of the German business register. This would mean less expenditure and smaller delays for those who want to obtain registration as well as for those who want to retrieve information on a company. Furthermore, he calls for a less time-consuming bureaucracy, which, at the same time, should keep a constant performance standard (Gernoth 2004, 840). For Kögel, the German legal practice is an impediment that can not last over time, if it is evaluated along the ECJ's standards. Hence, the matter is controversial even for domestic companies (Kögel 2004, 1765).

7.2.5 Acceptancy

In contrast to the limited, the GmbH has a history of more than a hundred years in the German legal and economic systems. Anyone who deals with the GmbH is more or less familiar with it. However, the relationship the Germans have to the limited is somewhat different. Its peculiarities, advantages and disadvantages are familiar only to a minority of Germans. The existing literature is almost exclusively found in publications which specialize in law or economics. Consequently, there is still considerable ignorance and prejudice regarding the limited.

Especially small and medium-sized enterprises, who predominantly engage in business on a national or regional level, have to employ marketing techniques that ensure them a reputation as trustworthy market participants when choosing a foreign form of business organization. If the enterprise does not ensure the needed transparency itself, its business partners are compelled to gather the relevant information. To obtain reliable information abroad demands a considerable amount of time and money, and possible language barriers stand in the way (Wachter 2004, 92 (a)).

7.3 Chances and Perspectives of the Limited

The sudden surge of limited establishments does not seem to be diminishing any time soon. Nevertheless, two inter-crossing developments may slow this development down a bit.

One of these, is the time limit of 22 months for the submittal of annual accounts in England (cp. Item 5.8.3), which will soon expire for the first, courageous founders of limiteds after the "Inspire Art"-decision in 2003. The first annual accounts of newly established limiteds with administrative seats in Germany must be submitted to the Companies House in Cardiff within the next 10 month after the end of the financial year, i.e. 22 month after the establishment. Hence, those who have established a limited directly or shortly after the "Inspire Art"-decision have to fulfil this duty now. Dierksmeier believes many founders of limiteds will be surprised as to what the costs for advice and bookkeeping will be. Some may even come to regret their decision in establishing a limited (Dierksmeier 2005, 1516).

The other development relates to the reduction of minimum capital, which has been announced for January $1^{st,}$ 2006. It results from a government draft of a law to amend the minimum capital of a GmbH (MindestKapG), brought in on June 16, 2005 and decided on by the federal cabinet on January 1st, 2005 (Dierksmeier 2005, 1516). Accordingly, the GmbH's minimum capital is set to be reduced to € 10,000. Moreover, the introduction of the electronic registration of companies (cp. item 7.2.4), is supposed to allow for the establishment of a GmbH within a matter of days (Dierksmeier 2005, 1521). Through this, the federal government attempts to adopt to the increasing number of the founders of limiteds, as well as to the increased demand in "discount-GmbHs".

The former two developments will then accordingly lead to the decreasing popularity of the limited, according to Dierksmeier and reverse the statistics in favour of the GmbH (Dierksmeier 2005, 1517).

However, Wand warns against welcoming these developments all too fast. He states that such a reform generates a fictitious security, and that it will, in fact, hardly decrease potential competition to the GmbH. Additionally, he calls for "1-Euro-

GmbHs" and law reformations on equitable subordination [Kapitalersatzrecht] and Cash-Pooling[9]. Furthermore, he advocates a mandatory authentication of the assignment of shares in a GmbH (Wand 2005, 1018).

Moreover, Wand maintains that the wave of establishments of limiteds may decrease as soon as the first corporate veil of a limited is lifted (Wand 2005, 1018).

Whether or not this wave will die down a bit or not will become more evident throughout the next few months, especially after the first of January of the upcoming year.

---

[9] "Cash-Pooling" in a group means an internal clearance of liquidity by a central financial management, in which the companies in the group are offered credits for the coverage of cash shortages. The pool is filled by cash surpluses of all the companies of the group.

8. Conclusion

With the series of decisions in the "Centros –", "Überseering –" and especially in the "Inspire Art" case, the ECJ has paved the way for unbound competition among the various European forms of business organization. The ECJ has clarified that freedom of establishment within the European Union - as guaranteed by the European treaty - may not be hampered by a single Member State's excessive restrictions. Restrictions concerning foreign companies are allowed only under the ECJ's framework of the "four-criteria-test". Due to this, a founder of a company has the option of setting up business in another potentially attractive EU Member State, in which he believes the business will profit the most. He is then free to engage in business throughout the Community and establish branch offices there.

Among other forms of business organizations, the British limited, which has come to serve as an alternative to founders who intend to set up a company with limited liability in Germany. The number of such establishments is estimated to have increased to more than 12,000 since March 2003 (Vogel 2005, 215). It is the fast and unbureaucratic establishment, achievable without huge financial expenses, that makes the limited seem very attractive. What's more, the English law does not demand a minimum share capital of € 25,000. In addition to deposits and non-cash contributions, services are also admissible as contributions in England. The management of a limited is assumed by directors who have been appointed by the general meeting, while the company secretary discharges the company's duties regarding the English Companies House. The assignment of shares is possible even informally and does not require a notarial authentication.

The fact that the management of a Ltd. amounts to additional costs and duties that are unheard of the establishment of a GmbH, is either accounted for or totally neglected. Current costs include the maintenance of the registered office in England, and the position of company secretary which must be assumed by one of the directors or by a professional third party. The English law also emphasises the maintenance of capital and the compliance to complicated rules concerning disclosure. If the due date for the disclosure of certain documents, as, for example, the annual accounts or annual return is exceeded, considerable fines, or even deregistration of the company are possible threats to the business. In England, a distribution to shareholders may be financed only by the limited's profits. A reduction in the amount of capital is possible only in the case of appeal to an English court. This results in a greater need for advice than would normally be necessary in the establishment of a GmbH.

Legal uncertainty remains problematic, especially with regard to the German concepts of liability in creditor protection, and boosts up the costs for English legal advice. It is still unclear as to what extent German law is applicable on foreign companies that are residents of Germany. However, one sure thing is that German tax law, in conjunction with the double taxation agreement between Great Britain and the Federal Republic of Germany, is applicable for limiteds that operate exclusively in Germany.

In order to engage in business with a limited in Germany the establishment of a branch office is advocated, although registration in the German register of companies is rather complicated and expensive.

It may be inferred that there is no substantial disadvantage for the limited when borrowing outside capital, since banks and creditors tend to rely more on the business concept and profit prospects of a company than on its equity.

If the advantages and drawbacks of the establishment of a firm in England, in comparison to the German GmbH, are evaluated, then it becomes clear that these factors speak in favour of the GmbH. Establishing a limited is logical only if the company intends to engage in business abroad and wishes for a good reputation, since the limited is favoured in most countries. The limited also makes sense as a short-term project, because the additional, current costs of compliance with the English accounting regulations outweigh the advantages in the long run. If the activities of the prospective company take place exclusively in Germany, the GmbH seems to be the smarter choice.

The final decision for, or against, the establishment of a domestic branch office is, however, dependent on the respective individual case. Nevertheless, the advantages and disadvantages that have been stated above, as well as the costs and duties, should always be accounted for, in order for any potential founder to correctly evaluate his chances and risks in the foundation of a "limited".

The reforms of the GmbH's minimum capital and the introduction of an electronic register in Germany still remain to be seen. By that time, however, it may be that the inconvenience of choosing a business organization form no longer occurs.

Annex 1

10

Please complete in typescript,
or in bold black capitals.
CHWP000
Notes on completion appear on final page

First directors and secretary and intended situation of registered office

Company Name in full

Proposed Registered Office
(PO Box numbers only, are not acceptable)

Post town

County / Region Postcode

If the memorandum is delivered by an agent for the subscriber(s) of the memorandum mark the box opposite and give the agent's name and address.

Agent'sName

Address

Post town

County / Region Postcode

Number of continuation sheets attached

You do not have to give any contact information in the box opposite but if you do, it will help Companies House to contact you if there is a query on the form. The contact information that you give will be visible to searchers of the public record.

Tel

DX number   DX exchange

Companies House receipt date barcode
This form has been provided free of charge by Companies House

When you have completed and signed the form please send it to the Registrar of Companies at:
Companies House, Crown Way, Cardiff, CF14 3UZ DX 33050 Cardiff
for companies registered in England and Wales or
Companies House, 37 Castle Terrace, Edinburgh, EH1 2EB
for companies registered in Scotland   DX 235 Edinburgh
or LP - 4 Edinburgh 2

v 08/02

Annex 2 12

Declaration on application for registration

Please complete in typescript, or in bold black capitals. CHWP000

Company Name in full

I,

of

† Please delete as appropriate.

do solemnly and sincerely declare that I am a † [Solicitor engaged in the formation of the company][person named as director or secretary of the company in the statement delivered to the Registrar under section 10 of the Companies Act 1985] and that all the requirements of the Companies Act 1985 in respect of the registration of the above company and of matters precedent and incidental to it have been complied with.

And I make this solemn Declaration conscientiously believing the same to be true and by virtue of the Statutory Declarations Act 1835.

Declarant's signature

Declared at

On   Day Month   Year

• Please print name.   before me •

Signed   Date

† A Commissioner for Oaths or Notary Public or Justice of the Peace or Solicitor

You do not have to give any contact information in the box opposite but if you do, it will help Companies House to contact you if there is a query on the form. The contact information that you give will be visible to searchers of the public record.

Tel

DX number   DX exchange

Companies House receipt date barcode

This form has been provided free of charge by Companies House.

Form revised 10/03

When you have completed and signed the form please send it to the Registrar of Companies at:
Companies House, Crown Way, Cardiff, CF14 3UZ DX 33050 Cardiff
for companies registered in England and Wales
or
Companies House, 37 Castle Terrace, Edinburgh, EH1 2EB
for companies registered in Scotland   DX 235 Edinburgh
or LP - 4 Edinburgh 2

Bibliography:

Reference Books:

Degenhardt, Klaus: *Die „Ltd." in Deutschland*, Salzwasser-Verlag, Bremen 2003.

Dierksmeier, Jochen: *Der Kauf einer englischen „Private Limited Company"*, Verlag für Recht und Wirtschaft, 1997.

Goldstein, Elmar/ Wulferding, Klaus: *Euro-GmbH – So setzen Sie eine englische Limited in Deutschland ein*, Goyang Media Ltd. Verlag 2004.

Güthoff, Julia: *Gesellschaftsrecht in Großbritannien*, first edition. München 1993.

Just, Clemens: *Die englische Limited in der Praxis*, Verlag C. H. Beck München, 2005.

Korts, Sebastian: *Die Europäische Kapitalgesellschaft (& Co. KG) am Beispiel einer Limited (& Co. KG)*, Verlag Recht und Wirtschaft Heidelberg 2004.

Scamell, Ernest. H.: *Lindley on the law of partnership*, twelfth edition, Sweet & Maxwell Ltd, London, 1962.

Triebel, Volker/ Hodgson, Stephen/ Kellenter, Wolfgang: *Englisches Handels- und Wirtschaftsrecht*, second edition, Heidelberg 1995.

Trade Journals:

Altmeppen, Holger: *Schutz vor „europäischen" Kapitalgesellschaften*, in: NJW 2/2004, pp. 97 – 104.

Bauhoff, Michael: *Sind englische Limited-Gesellschaften eine Alternative zur deutschen GmbH?*, in: WStH 19/2004, pp. 825 – 830.

Bayer, Walter: *Aktuelle Entwicklungen im Europäischen Gesellschaftsrecht*, in BB 1/2004, pp. 1 – 11.

Bayer, Walter: *Die EuGH-Entscheidung „Inspire Art" und die deutsche GmbH im Wettbewerb der europäischen Rechtsordnungen*, in BB 45/2003, pp. 2357 – 2365.

Dierksmeier, Jochen: *Die englische Limited in Deutschland – Haftungsrisiko in Deutschland*, in: BB 28/2005, pp. 1516 – 1523.

Ebert, Sabine/ Levedag, Christian: *Die zugezogene „private company limited by shares (Ltd.)" nach dem Recht von England und Wales als Rechtsformalternative für in- und ausländische Investoren in Deutschland*, in: GmbHR 22/2003, pp. 1337 – 1346.

Gernoth, Jan P.: *Das deutsche Handelsregister – telekommunikative Steinzeit im Zeichen des europäischen Wettbewerbs*, in: BB 16/2004, pp. 837 – 844.

Graf von Bernstorff, Christoph: *Das Betreiben einer englischen Limited in Deutschland*, in RIW 7/2004, pp. 498 – 502.

Happ, Wilhelm/ Holler, Lorenz: *"Limited" statt GmbH? Risiken und Kosten werden gern verschwiegen*, in DStR 17/2004, pp. 730 – 736.

Höreth, Ulrike/ Schiegl, Brigitte: *Die „Limited" – Rechtsform der Zukunft. Löst die Limited in Deutschland die GmbH ab?*, in: Steuer Transparent – Ernst & Young 2004, pp. 3 – 12.

Horn, Norbert: *Deutsches und europäisches Gesellschaftsrecht und die EuGH-Rechtsprechung zur Niederlassungsfreiheit – Inspire Art*, in NJW 13/2004, pp. 893 – 901.

Kallmeyer, Harald: *Vor- und Nachteile der englischen Limited im Vergleich zur GmbH oder GmbH & Co. KG*, in: DB 12/2004, pp. 636 – 639.

Kersting, Christian/ Schindler, Clemens Philipp: *Die EuGH-Entscheidung „Inspire Art" und ihre Auswirkungen auf die Praxis*, in RdW 11/2003, pp. 621 – 625.

Kögel, Steffen: *Formalien der GmbH-Gründung – ein Musterbeispiel für zuviel Staat*, in: GmbHR, 21/2003, pp. 1225 – 1230.

Kögel, Steffen: *Gründung einer ausländischen Briefkastenfirma: Wann ist eine Zweigniederlassung in Deutschland eine Zweigniederlassung?*, in: DB 33/2004, pp. 1763 – 1766.

Maul, Silja/ Schmidt, Claudia: *Inspire Art – Quo Vadis Sitztheorie?*, in BB 44/2003, pp. 2297 – 2300.

Meilicke, Wienand: Der GmbHR-Kommentar zu: *Errichtung einer Zweigniederlassung in einem anderen EU-Mitgliedstaat*, in: GmbHR 21/2003, pp. 1260 – 1271.

Pannen, Klaus/ Riedemann, Susanne: *Checkliste: Die Englische „Ltd." mit Verwaltungssitz in Deutschland in der Insolvenz*, in: MDR 9/2005, pp. 496 – 498.

Probst, Peter/ Kleinert, Jens: *Erneut klare Absage an Wegzugbeschränkungen durch EuGH und Kommission*, in NJW 34/2004, pp. 2425 – 2439.

Probst, Peter/ Kleinert, Jens: *Schein-Auslandsgesellschaften - Erneute Betonung der Niederlassungsfreiheit durch den EuGH*, in MDR 22/2003, pp. 1265 – 1268.

Riedemann, Susanne: *Das Auseinanderfallen von Gesellschafts- und Insolvenzstatut – „Inspire Art" und die Insolvenz über das Vermögen einer englischen „limited" in Deutschland*, in GmbHR 6/2004, pp. 345 – 349.

Riegger, Bodo: *Centros – Überseering – Inspire Art: Folgen für die Praxis*, in ZGR 3-4/ 2004, pp. 510 – 530.

Schumann, Alexander: *Die englische Limited mit Verwaltungssitz in Deutschland: Kapitalaufbringung, Kapitalerhaltung und Haftung bei Insolvenz*, in: DB 14/2004, pp. 743 – 749.

Spindler, Gerald/ Berner, Olaf: *Der Gläubigerschutz im Gesellschaftsrecht nach Inspire Art*, in RIW 1/2004, pp. 7 – 16.

Süß, Rembert: *Muß die Limited sich vor Gründung einer Ltd. & Co. KG in das deutsche Handelsregister eintragen lassen?*, in: GmbHR 11/2005, pp. 673 – 674.

Triebel, Volker/ von Hase, Karl: *Wegzug und grenzüberschreitende Umwandlungen deutscher Gesellschaften nach „Überseering" und „Inspire Art"*, in BB 46/2003, pp. 2409 – 2417.

Vogel, Hans-Gert: *Eine neue Gesellschaftsform wird populär – Unternehmensgründer wählen immer häufiger die britische Limited*, in Betriebswirtschaftliche Blätter 4/2005, pp. 211 – 215.

Von Halen, Curt Christian: *Das internationale Gesellschaftsrecht nach dem Überseering-Urteil des EuGH*, in WM 12/2003, pp. 571 – 578.

w/o author, 2005 (a): *Anmeldung: Eintragung der Befreiung vom Selbstkontrahierungsverbot in das Handelsregister für die Zweigniederlassung einer englischen Limited Company*, in: GmbHR 3/2005, pp. 168 – 172.

w/o author, 2005 (b): *Der Gläubigerschutz bei Auslandsgesellschaften im Gefolge der aktuellen EuGH-Rechtsprechung*, in: INF 4/2005, pp. 151 – 156.

Wachter, Thomas, 2004 (a): *Auswirkungen des EuGH-Urteils in Sachen Inspire Art Ltd. auf Beratungspraxis und Gesetzgebung – Deutsche GmbH vs. englische private limited company*, in GmbHR, 2/2004, pp. 88 – 105.

Wachter, Thomas, 2004 (b): *Handelsregisteranmeldung der inländischen Zweigniederlassung einer englischen Private Limited Company*, in MDR 11/2004, pp. 611 – 619.

Wachter, Thomas: *Errichtung, Publizität, Haftung und Insolvenz von Zweigniederlassungen ausländischer Kapitalgesellschaften nach „Inspire Art"*, in GmbHR 21/2003, pp. 1254 – 1257.

Wachter, Thomas: *Wettbewerb des GmbH-Rechts in Europa*, in GmbHR 12/2005, pp. 717 – 730.

Wand, Peter: *Europa-/Gesellschaftsrecht: Persönliche Haftung des Geschäftsführers einer private limited company mit Verwaltungssitz in Deutschland für rechtsgeschäftliche Gesellschaftsverbindlichkeiten?*, in BB 19/2005, pp. 1016 – 1018.

Werner, Heinz: *Euro-Gmbhs fast ohne Limits: Erfolgsmodell englische Limited*, in: Mein Geld – Kapital und Börsenblatt 5-6/ 2004, pp. 49 – 54.

Werner, Rüdiger: *Die Ltd. & Co. KG – eine Alternative zur GmbH & Co. KG?*, in: GmbHR 5/2005, pp. 288 – 294.

Figures:

Triebel, Volker: *Warum englische LTD oder PLC statt deutscher GmbH oder AG?* zu finden: http://www.dihk.de/inhalt/download/ltd_triebel.pdf.

Festschriften:

Heinz, Volker: *Englische Limited und Deutsche GmbH – eine vergleichende Darstellung*, vorgetragen am 21.5.2004 auf dem 55. Deutschen Anwaltstag in Hamburg, pp. 1 – 35.

Internet Sources:

Bartsch, Holger: *Ist die englische Limited wirklich eine Alternative zur GmbH*, 2005 found:
www.stade.ihk24.de/STDIHK24/STDIHK24/produktmarken/index.jsp?url=http%3A//www.stade.ihk24.de/STDIHK24/STDIHK24/produktmarken/recht_und_fair_play/Europarecht/Limited12951.jsp , 08/13/05.

Go Ahead Limited: *Die Limited Company – „In der Übersicht"*, found: www.go-limited.de/Download/Download_von_Infos.shtml , 05/27/05.

www.encyclopedia.com/html/M/MuscovyC1.asp , 08/17/05 (a).

www.ex.ac.uk/~RDavies/arian/amser/chrono6.html , 08/17/05.

http://en.wikipedia.org/wiki/Joint_Stock_company , 08/17/05 (a).

www.encyclopedia.com/html/s/sths1eab1.asp , 08/17/05 (b).

http://en.wikipedia.org/wiki/Bubble_act , 08/17/05 (b).

www.hmrc.gov.uk/manuals/intmanual/INTM120150.htm , 08/17/05 (a).

www.bbc.co.uk/history/timelines/england/vic_limited_liabilities_act.shtml , 08/17/05.

www.hmrc.gov.uk/manuals/intmanual/INTM120150.htm , 08/17/05 (b).

www.hmrc.gov.uk/manuals/svmanual/svm02010.htm , 08/17/05 (c).

www.hmrc.gov.uk/manuals/svmanual/svm02010.htm , 08/17/05 (d).

www.companieshouse.gov.uk/about/functionsHistory.shtml , 08/17/05 (a).

http://de.wikipedia.org/wiki/Niederlassungsfreiheit , 06/23/05.

www.companieshouse.gov.uk/about/guidence.shtml , 06/24/05 (b).